Building After Katrina: Visions for the Gulf Coast
edited by Betsy Roettger

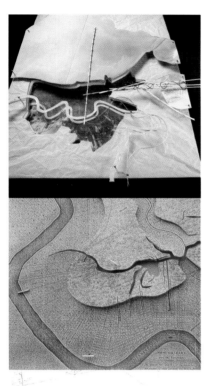

URGENT MATTERS vol. 2
The University of Virginia School of Architecture

cover images from the top, by:
Betsy Roettger
Katherine Floersheimer
Anne Bohlen
ecoMOD design/build studio
Justin Laskin and Kathleen Mark
JP Mays
Jordan Phemister, main cover image

07 06 05 04 03 02 01 7654321 First Edition

ISBN 978-0-9771024-5-7

ISSN 1556-5483

Book design: Kevin Bell, Erin Hannegan, and Betsy Roettger
Printed by Carter Printing, Richmond, VA
Distributed by the University of Virginia Press

University of Virginia School of Architecture
Campbell Hall, P.O. Box 400122
Charlottesville, VA 22904
www.arch.virginia.edu

editor's notes

As I left the school of architecture today to take our files to the publisher, I passed a graduating student, Ben Thompson, presenting a sophisticated design research scheme, representing a year of study looking at rebuilding a school and neighborhood in New Orleans. Anselmo Canfora, an architecture faculty member, and his students were presenting their research and design development of disaster relief emergency and transitional housing prototypes. Just last week, one our landscape architecture faculty, Julie Bargmann, exhibited ongoing work in New Orleans, called the "Big Mud", looking at de-tox-ing and rebuilding the soil base that has been stripped away by the flooding.

These recent projects reminded me that is has been a full year since the work represented in this book was submitted last spring semester. Since that time, many students and faculty have continued their work in the Gulf Coast through design efforts, serving on various commissions, and traveling frequently to collaborate with non-profits' efforts in the area. We could publish another volume on the breath of studies being done in the New Orleans area and similar work being pursued around the world. For now, we offer one semester's work to communicate the pedagogical values of our school, to contribute case studies for applied design research, and to present innovative strategies for re-building to the Gulf Coast communities.

For a school of architecture devoted to learning through public service, this disaster and the resulting collaborative work in the school marked a strengthening of our long term commitment to incorporating "urgent matters" into the curriculum. The current generation of design students represent an evolution of the design process from one focused on a singular author, site, and program to a process that embraces much larger ideas of site and cultural systems. Many of the proposed schemes presented in the book are based on community and ecological restoration over time through a mutual re-building of natural and man-made systems. This new design methodology and interest by the students, is promoting the idea of design leadership and pushing designers to explore alternative methods of practicing architecture and landscape architecture.

While this is a critical time for the future of the Gulf Coast communities, the work in this publication is applicable to global design problems. How does one design an intervention for a specific culture, ecology, and time? How do we respond to both disaster relief and long term restoration? How does the design profession advance work at the intersection of disciplines? How do we propose designs that improve the environmental underpinnings of a place while serving the many cultures that shape public space? And how can the role of the design professional become an essential voice in shaping policies that affect our physical and cultural landscape?

Betsy Roettger, Editor

I would especially like to thank the designers, Kevin Bell, M Arch 2006 for getting us started and Erin Hannegan, M Arch 2008 for the tenacity to keep the process going. Thank you to the many players that supported this publication: University of Virginia Arts Council; Karen Van Legen, Dean, School of Architecture, University of Virginia; William Sherman, Associate Professor and Chair, Department of Architecture & Landscape Architecture; Alice Keys, Assistant to the Dean; Derry Wade, Director of Publications; and Elizabeth Fortune, Associate Dean for Administration and Finance. Also, thank you to the students and faculty who contributed work, those outside the school who supported travel, my family, especially Bob Pineo, and to the non-profits and residents of the Gulf Coast region who welcomed us into their lives.

preface

The University of Virginia, since its founding in 1824 by Thomas Jefferson, has supported a public mandate to educate and develop our democratic culture. As part of this larger mission, the School of Architecture focuses on analysis and design in the public realm, in support of architectures of democracy. Just as a democratic culture is a dialogue and cooperative effort of individuals; analysis and design in the public realm is a discussion and joint effort of individual disciplines working collaboratively to investigate and propose aesthetic, humanistic and ecologically intelligent outcomes.

This book and its representative work come directly out of this ethic and bears witness to this school's comprehensive involvement in the aftermath of Hurricane Katrina. Two powerful historical events have marked the beginning of this 21st century: the terrorist attacks of September 11, 2001 and Hurricane Katrina in August of 2005: one a human-inspired disaster, the other a natural disaster. The effects of both of these events will be felt in many ways for years to come and will certainly change the temperament of our culture. We are a school committed to creative solutions that might stimulate positive changes in new and thoughtful ways.

Hurricane Katrina, one of the country's worst natural disasters, resulted in over 1300 deaths and an estimated 81 billion dollars in damage, including the loss of thousands of homes, schools and businesses leaving an entire region of our country broken and severely damaged. The hurricane could not have been prevented but the region was not sufficiently prepared to withstand a natural disaster of this magnitude. The government's lackluster performance in coping with all of the phases of this disaster, from infrastructural design and maintenance to rescue and restoration, has been even more tragic and has laid bare the incompetence of so many levels of our government and public processes.

It is in this context that our School of Architecture decided to proactively offer our ideas and our expertise to the reconstruction efforts throughout the Gulf region. We sent many students and faculty to the region to help in the clean-up efforts. We co-sponsored a January term course to comprehensively evaluate the complexity of the failures, including the engineering/infrastructural problems, the political aspects as well as the resultant human and social ramifications. However, our largest effort was a school-wide collective response in which half of our design studios in the Department of Architecture and Landscape Architecture took on the problems of the region offering analytical studies along with new ideas and strategies for repairing and rebuilding this region. Our Planning and History of Architecture faculty offered background and analysis for this work and generously lectured on these aspects to the larger University and region.

I am very proud as the Dean of this School of Architecture to present these projects to the public in the interest of aiding that ongoing process of recovery and in strategically offering new solutions that range in scale from infrastructural planning and regional landscapes to the scale of the neighborhood. We worked together as a united community to share our expertise and our values and this book represents that moment in our school's history.

Karen Van Lengen
Dean and Edward E. Elson Professor of Architecture

contents

1

As the media covered the tragedy taking place on the ground along the Gulf Coast and on the roofs of New Orleans after Hurricane Katrina, it was as if the country was stunned into immediate mourning. We had seen many natural disasters unleashed around the world and had been moved to re-build the places and people's lives that were destroyed, but something was different about the way people responded to the aftermath of Hurricane Katrina. Along with this deep sense of mourning for the people and families who were lost, there were feelings of anger, apprehension, and fear that one of the most unique cultures left in our country was gone forever.

For those of us who live in other parts of the country, New Orleans and the areas along the Gulf Coast have a certain mystique to them. As both the nation and world become more homogenized, these are the places that remain in our fantasy as more spiritual, more diverse, more artistic, more alive with history, more tied to their climate and landscape; more based on place. While we watched the events unfold after the hurricane, we were enraged at the inhumane treatment of the citizens of this special place while we began to mourn the loss of a treasured culture. Of course, much of the charisma of the New Orleans and Gulf Coast must be balanced with the darker side to the region based in poverty, corruption, and plagued by crime. With the exposure of this level of poverty in our country, there was a shock at the ever growing chasm between the upper and lower classes in the United States. In part, the urge to travel to the region and offer help was based on serving who would now be pushed deeper into the class of people just getting by before the hurricane and who now had nothing. There was another calling to go to the region, to mourn the loss of a culture, like the need to go to a funeral for someone you didn't really know but greatly admired. Lastly, as those anxious about the rebuilding process, we had to see the "new site" or current context for ourselves.

As designers, we work at a crossroads. We work at the intersection between the many visible physical systems which determine how spaces are built and we work within the invisible systems; the economic, political, and social aspects of what gets built. More and more, our profession has been expanding beyond the intersection between these two systems and trying to engage in both worlds more fully. Through expanding our role as designers, we offer a voice much earlier in the conversation and do not wait until someone hands over the "problem", the parameters of the project, to the designer to solve. For example, as designers are more involved in the physical aspects of setting up a building project, they are better able to choose appropriate sites based on the unique ecologies of the land, take time to engage the existing context of a community, and question the program before it is handed to them - what is to be built and why? Thinking about the more invisible systems, designers can begin to question policies that shape what is allowed to be built. This upstream approach includes questioning zoning, density, ecology, potential for adding public spaces, transportation connections, and the ability to include the surrounding communities in the design process.

In observing the conditions on the ground four months after Katrina, we could observe all these complex systems, their intersections, and the effects of their failings. In their absence, the invisible systems became clearly visible. This book will not cover the complex unfolding history of the Gulf Coast region, but will offer design proposals based on moving forward in this new way of thinking about the integration of people, ecology, and building.

photos show the new ad hoc method of communication found the Gulf Coast

I cannot think of a better way for students to learn about the complex networks that make up a place than to work and live in a city that has lost all its physical, social, governmental, landscape, economic, and community infrastructure. This was the reality we entered in early January 2006. In addition to facing a situation unprecedented in its scope of devastation, the students also learned, by necessity, skills that are essential for a both designers and leaders. These skills are often overlooked in traditional academic architectural training but are essential given this shift in the role of the design professional. Instead of acting as individual lead designers, the students had to work collaboratively, be creative in their use of available tools to solve problems, remain very flexible, navigate without infrastructure, and thoughtfully access the situation by listening and communicating very carefully with residents. Before even thinking about design and building, there needed to be a process for listening and thinking critically about not just rebuilding but rethinking.

As a group, our first sight entering New Orleans on Interstate 10, once the wealthiest and third largest city in our country, was a lack of any visibility - it was complete darkness. We quickly realized the effects of electricity not being restored to 80% of the city. As we descended into the city, we could see remnants of the infrastructural systems that made up the city, occasional street signs, recognizable monuments and known divisions between neighborhoods, but all signs of life, normal daily routines, and typical standards for navigating the area had been erased. It seemed as if we inhabited miles and miles of a museum after hours or an uninhabited archeological dig. We were looking at artifacts that described a civilization now lost. This condition was a bit different as we drove along the Gulf Coast as there were only foundations and strong live oaks left to mark where buildings once were, as if the museum had remained but was now empty of artifacts. We later learned that four months after the hurricanes, there were only about 25% of the citizens living back in the region.

In our contemporary society, we are used to communicating, navigating, and receiving needed services instantly. Without any infrastructure, we rapidly learned new ways of working that included having to plan every meal, access to water, restrooms, and the ability to find our way. For example, the lack of signage, street lights, and people led to an ad hoc method of communication. Signage lined the streets advertising construction and gutting services while personal notes were spray painted on houses to and from families who had no other way of being in contact. Of course the most personal of the signage we read as we drove through the streets, were the markings painted onto every structure by the various agencies, the local police, FEMA, and the insurance companies. Although the neighborhoods were completely empty of residents, we knew when their house was entered, how many people had lived there, how many bodies had been found, how many animals were found dead or alive, and what level of toxic waste and water remained and, in some cases, a status for entry or potential rebuilding.

As we worked in neighborhoods and gutted homes, we felt as if we were getting to know the families through all their now ruined belongings. It was a strange feeling to occupy homes and neighborhoods that were completely empty but full of personal debris. Places that may have had serious crime problems felt completely safe, operating in a city without people started to feel almost normal, although we did leave our work at sunset when the city fell into total darkness. Anyone we did meet that had returned to their communities seemed grateful and welcoming to all who were there to help. They also were eager to share their frustrations and stories, especially because they could not yet make decisions or discuss their future. Because the policies for rebuilding were not in place, they could only access damage, being to clean up, wait, and worry.

Meeting residents of varying income levels and the local organizers providing assistance gave us insight into the failing of the government and the insurance companies to make decisions. No matter a person's race or financial standing, they had to wait. This was in early January, four full months after the disaster, and residents did not know if they would receive money from their insurance policies, if their neighborhoods would be allowed to rebuild, or even how the process of decision-making would include them or when it would happen.

above: The worst damage in the city of New Orleans occurred where the Industrial Canal was breached in the lower ninth ward neighborhood.

right: photos from the first public meeting of the mayor's "Bring Back New Orleans Commission"

As we worked, we learned the subtleties of the language presented by FEMA to describe a family's potential to rebuild. With a quick inspection, FEMA would indicate the percentage of damage done to the house; 50% or less meant you might receive money to rebuild (if the city designated your neighborhood for rebuilding), over 50% damaged meant that you might not receive financial assistance, the ability to obtain a building permit, or even be offered tarps to shelter what remained of your property. Of course, another obvious problem with FEMA's, seemingly subjective, assistance strategy could be seen in or not seen in the placement of the FEMA trailers. Without any water or electricity to hook up to, the only FEMA trailers we saw within the city of New Orleans were in neighborhoods with little infrastructural damage. This allowed only a small portion of the population to be able to return for an overnight stay in order to access their damage, attend meetings, and question the damage assessments for their property.

While attending the first presentation by the mayor's "Bring Back New Orleans Commission", it was clear that the residents did not feel that the government meant to serve them, or was in fact listening to their concerns. Residents were trying to live in or return to a city where there was no water, no electricity, no food, no health care, no city services, no schools, no public transportation, no sense of government or structure to the city, limited shelter, and no plan for the piles and piles of waste that engulfed the city. They wanted to know how to live - how to plan their next steps and future. Their frustration was palpable as they were presented with far-reaching plans of mixed use development and high speed rail systems that might affect improve the quality of life in ten to twenty years, without discussion of their current situation.

It was obvious that enraged residents wanted more immediate answers when shown the tentative layouts for the city's reorganization. Zones for development were overlaid onto the city map showing levels of potential rebuilding for neighborhoods. These zones ranged from neighborhoods with no rebuilding at all, neighborhoods that would be turned into parks, those that could rebuild and remain, to neighborhoods where large swaths of mega redevelopment would obliterate the existing communities. In seeing the plans, the fear did not stem as much from the loss of physical neighborhoods, but that the displaced communities, many who had lived together for generations, would not have a place or the ability to return in the proposed reorganization. Who would make up this new city?

making the invisible visible | betsy roettger

7

*below: framing a "house in a box"
with Habitat for Humanity in Charlottesville, VA*

photos show the living conditions for volunteers and returning residents

As volunteers trying to do the most we could with our time, we could only get a taste of what it would be like to be a resident of the City of New Orleans or someone along the Gulf Coast going through a similar waiting game. For the time being, we, and most of those we encountered, were living almost exclusively off the generosity of others and our own contributions. As we worked in the city, we found ways to work with donated tools, relying on non-profits' generators for power and water, found donated food and clothing, and in one case - donated healthcare.

Surprisingly, we did not find visible government check points or stations offering help, although one large national organization, the Red Cross, dropped off lunches one day, and we did occasionally see military trucks patrolling the area. What we did notice were many small grassroots groups out in the streets offering their services. We found that if you took the time to talk with people, you could find warm meals, clothing, and healthcare offered for free without any paperwork or questions. On the other hand, the one government-sponsored tent I approached, in search of socks so the students could shed their mold-ridden shoes, would not let me enter as I did not have appropriate papers from that particular neighborhood.

It is in the pro-active, grassroots and non-profit organizations that New Orleans and the surrounding region must hold hope for rebuilding their communities. We came upon many people who had come down to volunteer and were not doing the heroic activities they had expected to perform. In the suburb of Chalmette, we met with an organization living in tents on a parking lot. They were preparing and serving 1000 healthy meals a day for free - with smiles on their faces. This diverse group of people from all over the country did not expect that this is what the community would need, but with volunteers arriving to gut houses and no restaurants or services, they were working 14-hour days creating a new community. These were the positive stories - the places where a simple meal or just a hand-washing station would lead to discussions and show the life that was returning to the city. In the suburbs, some chain restaurants, with more ability to rebound than the local businesses, were trying to open. Places like McDonald's and Burger King were offering $5,000 signing bonuses trying to find staff, but even with these opening, there was a real lack of healthy food available.

We learned as much about the clean-up of a disaster this enormous as we did about the power of these grassroots organizations to keep the base essentials for life available for those willing to return to the area. The people we were able to work with were inspiring in their hope and visions for the places they were trying to restore, but also for their sheer amount of work organizing an unknown amount of people coming either in need of assistance, or wanting to help from all over the country.

9

photos show working with Project Green
in Bay St. Louis, Mississippi

With a few phone calls, we were able to find shelter for the week, meals, supplies, tools, and places to work in different areas of the region. It will be these organizations with new efforts from universities and housing organizations that keep the area afloat and even moving forward until federal or local government agencies are funded and ready to offer clear decisions.

In Charlottesville, we had worked with Habitat for Humanity on their "house in a box" project so expected to continue that work with them in Louisiana. Habitat's large organization was doing its best to keep up with the huge demand to house volunteers willing to build. They were able to set us up with a church for food and shelter and a place to work in Slidell, Louisiana. There wasn't as much damage in some areas of Slidell so they could begin work on the "houses in boxes" that were being transported from other states around the country. Through the national press this program had received, there were a great many volunteers waiting to work which allowed us to explore other organizations in the area that were in more need of our time.

We then traveled along the Gulf Coast to Bay St. Louis, Mississippi and saw miles and miles of foundations left along the Gulf of Mexico. It was almost as if a different disaster struck outside the topographic bowl of New Orleans. The area was more ravished by the wind and storm surge leaving less of the original structures, more scattered debris, and even less in the way of signage or means of navigating.

We worked with one of the directors of Project Green, Dan Reynolds, on salvaging historic materials from his own property. His organization's goal was to save historic sites as much as possible by being involved in the gutting process in the hope of restoring the properties or recycling the materials. They had established Project Green before the hurricane as a center in New Orleans to recycle old valuable building materials and were quickly having to re-organize to serve as best they could with the tons of building materials that were being hauled away.

11

*photos show working with the Common Ground Collective
in the upper ninth ward neighborhood of New Orleans*

Within the city of New Orleans, we worked with the Common Ground Collective which proved to be the most forward thinking and politically active organization we found. Started with one man in a boat distributing water, by the time we were arrived, the Common Ground Collective had secured headquarters for volunteer work throughout the city. Only four months after Katrina, they were securing properties to expand their network, had set up free media centers, free law assistance, a free medical clinic (which we noticed was much needed as pharmacies were not open yet), plans for wetland restoration, community gardens, and were closely following the political situation so they could defend members of communities that were being evicted or were unable to return.

We worked mainly in the upper ninth ward gutting houses that through their agreement with Common Ground would then be used to shelter volunteer workers. Unlike the gutting we did in Mississippi, all materials left in New Orleans were considered toxic after sitting in the slurry of floodwaters for a month. The Common Ground Collective had a strong environmental agenda, so we tested alternative methods for bleaching the houses after they were gutted using microorganisms and molasses. One of the most impressive aspects of this organization was in the way it would take in volunteers, assign them a project and manager, run through all the safety precautions, and provide the needed gear; respirators, goggles, tyvek suits, boots, tools, delivered healthy meals, water, and organized the post-gutting clean up of volunteers and supplies.

13

January 7 – 14, 2006
volunteers

Betsy Roettger
Bob Pineo
John Quale
Christina Calabrese
Lauren Shirely
Paul Fromm
JP Mays
Katie Floersheimer
Greta Modesitt
Jordan Gravely
Adrienne Hicks
Jessica Foster
Graham Schnaars
Ravi Sarpatwari
Benjamin Kidd
Rosalyn Schmitt
Molly O'Donnell
Erin Binney
Emily Kappes
Melissa Elliot
Corey Barnes
Astrid Chastka

organizations

Habitat for Humanity, Charlottesville, VA
Northridge Baptist Church, Slidell, LA
Habitat for Humanity, Slidell, LA
Project Green
Common Ground Collective

Thank you to the financial
contributors who made this trip possible.

photos taken by Betsy Roettger and Molly O'Donnell

photos show gutting a house in on day in Chalmette, Lousisana

Our last experience with a gutting project was in the eastern suburb of Chalmette. We helped a family gut their parents' home that no one had entered since the flooding. This couple who had lived there were in their 80's and had no flood insurance so we were gutting down to the shell of the house for resale. In addition to the usual line of mold that had taken over the home following the floodwater level (here at 8 feet), there was also a heavy black sludge that had taken over the neighborhood from oil that spilled out of the nearby refineries. At that time, there had been no word on whether the oil companies would be offering assistance with the clean-up effort. We removed every belonging the couple owned along with most of the building material in the house. We watched the pile of trash raise to match the size of the house and wondered where it would go? As you drove through the area, the mounds of trash were unbelievable which again made us question the materials and process that would be used for rebuilding.

The observations made during our seven-day service trip go beyond describing what was lost; the extensive historic building fabric, entire communities, or any sounds and signs of life. As we began to understand the many layers of rebuilding infrastructure, ecologies, and social structure that would have to take place for people's return, we saw that our best skill was to listen and physically help sorting through what was left behind. This service work was an important step not only for those of us who went to understand the new context for building, but also to set the stage for design work. The remained of this book offers the school's design work, by students and faculty, working in the area over the following spring semester.

New Orleans fragile civic infrastructure was crushed by tons of floodwater. 180,000 returning residents find themselves trying to rebuild midst the city infrastructure that once supported a community of 500,000. Residents have no choice but to rethink and redesign their basic civic infrastructure that protects services and produces an active city. This course explores both conventional and emerging new directions in infrastructure thinking. The collaborative group of architecture, landscape architecture and planning students were asked to translate their research into a deck of playing cards. We were inspired to create these cards by Professor and landscape architect Jane Wolff's groundbreaking book and negotiation cards called Delta Primer. As in Wolff's book, these cards illustrate that the rebuilding of New Orleans neighborhoods and city requires an infrastructure that is a mixed hand of ecological, cultural, economic, and technological invention.

Our deck of cards is organized in the following manner. There are four suits of 13 cards each. The suits are Inaugural Terrain (IT), Second Nature (SN), Glocal Networks (GN), and Generative Hubs (GH). These combine to make a total deck of 52 cards. Each suit addressed the same set of rebuilding situations that represent the range of New Orleans rebuilding infrastructure questions. They are (civic support) Levees and Neutral Grounds, (basic services) Rebuilding Faubourgs and (sustainability) Elevation Green.

Class card design team:

Justin Aff, Jonah Chiarenza, Sara Downing, David Duxbury, Melissa Elliott, Margaret Fain, Megan Findley, Andrew Greene, Katie Jaeger, Andrea Lavin, Benjamin Mc Farlane, Mark Phemister, Maria Sanchez-Carlos, Tyler Schwartz, and Shannon Yadsko.

Refloat NOLA
"What's in the Cards for Rebuilding New Orleans Infrastructure"

william morrish

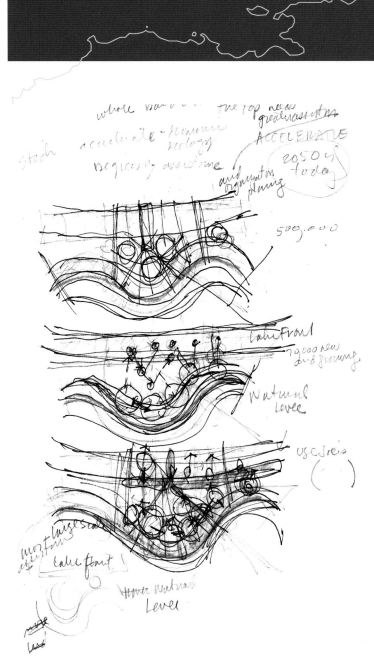

Searching the debris of broken lines and flooded networks for the threads of the New Orleans recovery civic infrastructure.

At dawn of August 29, 2005,

Hurricane Katrina roared ashore, battering the City of New Orleans and its neighboring Gulf Coast communities. The wind and the massive tidal surge ripped through the relaxed world of coastal Sunbelt cities leaving little behind but memories.

Returning to my former home to help family and colleagues sift through the human and physical debris, I found howling storm winds replaced by silence. People, birds and other signs of life had disappeared. All that remained of these active communities were fragments tossed about into piles of building foundations, cars, boats, toppled oaks, scattered family photos and mud-caked Mardi Gras beads. The disaster stripped away the veneer of carefree lifestyles of many on the Gulf Coast, most profoundly for those living in the City of New Orleans. The Crescent City was no longer operating in the age of "let the good times roll." Beyond having to face new risks of the global climate change and a more active weather cycle, this biblical storm opened a much larger cultural and societal question about the health, safety and welfare of our American cities. In New Orleans, the storm accelerated a cultural disaster that has been undermining the basic economic, social, and ecological infrastructure of New Orleans and many other American Cities for the last twenty years. Rebuilding New Orleans offers the country an opportunity to rethink our approach to building the civic infrastructure for the next generation of American cities.

EXPOSED FRAGILE FOUNDATION

New Orleans and Gulf Coast Cities are located in a historically dynamic ecological geography. For the last 30 years, we as a nation have supported the migration of our population away from urban centers in the north that were supported by years of infrastructure investment. As opposed to such cities as Chicago, New York and even Los Angeles, these cities do not have a long history of infrastructure development to support the complex cities they have become. They moved into Sunbelt cities and towns that only recently have begun to invest in the needed systems to support their size and complexity.

17

Sunbelt cities along the Gulf coast are small resort communities who have taken on large populations of families on fixed income. This population is a heavy user of infrastructure with little financial capacity to support new infrastructure at a time when there is little interest at the national level to underwrite these investments to serve more than major economic development interests such as casinos and industry.

Post-Katrina recovery clearly showed that many residents live on the edge of basic city services and safety. This weakness or fragile foundation leaves cities even more exposed to increased damage and profoundly decreases its ability to rebound after a natural and human disaster. In New Orleans, the collapse of its patchwork levee system flooding crushing its basic civic foundations service infrastructure networks translated Katrina's Category 3 force winds into Category 5 destruction. The City of New Orleans smaller population lives on top of the infrastructure carcass that once served a city double its size. Tons of floodwater sitting for weeks crushed the cities underground infrastructure systems along with the basic social safety and governance network to support dispersed neighborhood rebuilding efforts.

Today, the city of New Orleans barely floats above a service level of basic survival. For example, the City of New Orleans Water and Sewer Board pumps 125 million gallons of water into the crushed water supply lines, to deliver 40 million gallons of potable water to a much smaller population, 80 million gallons leak out through cracks in sidewalks and burrows under streets.

Though other American city infrastructure systems have not been crushed by floodwater, many are approaching a perilous threshold, under the weight of neglect and deferred maintenance. In New Orleans, the public dollar has been spent on tourist entertainment venues. But few of those dollars have trickled down to underpin the city's basic services. In an age of global competitiveness, infrastructure is not a national priority, but a complicated mosaic of systems operating as benevolent monopolies or autonomous enclaves. New Orleans reveals that our cities are situated on suspect systems. Infrastructure operators and civic oversight invest little in multi-functional infrastructure that supports global connectivity, the disenfranchised or resilience in the face of human and ecological catastrophe.

Refloating New Orleans provides other American cities with a national laboratory to explore new ways to design, operate, finance, and rebuild the infrastructure for the next generation of American cities responding to local, regional and global changes in a society of highly interconnected economic and ecological risks.

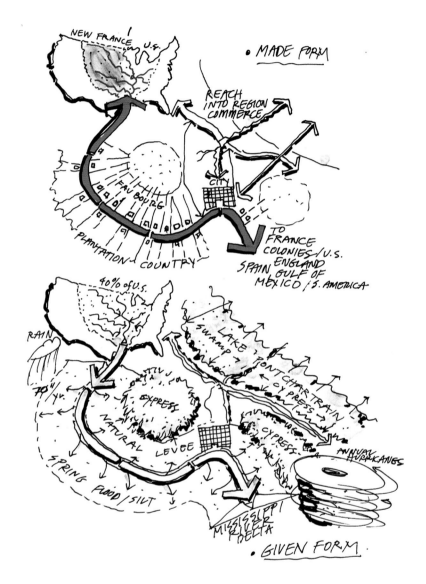

Inaugural Terrain

The storm and levee collapse has changed the ground upon which the city was founded and has grown up for over 200 years. It is no longer a city living behind levees, on sloping batture and upon dredged swamps, but within the cultural ecology of five diverse urban landscape basins each needing a different infrastructure to sustain itself within a wide range of risky terrains. This is a city learning to live on dynamic wet ground in a stormy world.

3,500,000 Trash Trucks?

Are we willing to use these trucks to clean up Katrina? The US Army Corps of Engineers estimates there are 22 million tons of waste in New Orleans and that choosing to remove all of it would require a line of garbage trucks 36,000 miles long. Certainly we aren't seriously considering this as a viable solution to the Katrina cleanup? Unfortunately, we are. So far, recycling efforts have been very limited. As for success stories, the effort to collect and recycle steel has so far yielded 280,000 tons. But thought of another way, this is about 1% of the estimated waste present. 25 million tons of vegetative waste have been dumped into local swamp/landfills or set fire. Other types of waste share a similar fate. Ruined computers, tvs, and other electronic devices contain metals and other hazardous materials that may leak and contaminate soil and groundwater. Much of the reusable building material, including rare cypress wood, is being sent to landfills rather than put to use in a city with a unprecedented high demand.

Islands of Leadership: The Role of Institutions

The devastation Hurricane Katrina caused created not only physical problems in the city and region, but instititional problems as well between the mayor's office, governor and FEMA. Without a clear plan or guiding force, action was forestalled as bureaucratic inertia slowed down recoverey efforts. In contrast, independent institutions such as the universities were able to **attack the problems** the hurricane left them with immediately because they were forced to. Planning for the new universities of the new New Orleans began the day the hurricane left. Taking action at this level created **islands of real leadership** that were not as obstructed as the various government agents were. Universities allied with each other to begin solving the problems addressing the city as a whole. This model of leadership suggests a greater role for institutions such as universities in the development of community leaders. Universities are no longer ivory towers walled off from their surroundings, but shining beacons that **lead by example.**

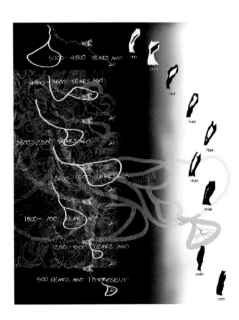

SOGGY ECONOMIC AND
ECOLOGICAL FOOTINGS

When the storm clouds cleared, satellite photos revealed that the storm surge had stripped away enough tidal grassland and trees equal to fifty years of what had been viewed as normal decay of wetlands of the Mississippi River delta.

The local urban ecology is framed by two natural systems – the Mississippi River and the urban forest canopy of live oaks. Both reveal the complex water regime that defines life in New Orleans, as more than river levee, pump and canal. It revealed that metropolitan New Orleans neighborhoods "stay above water" within a mosaic of five different drainage basins. Basins are urbanized sub-watersheds. Katrina's tidal surges demonstrated the exposure situation difference between each basin. Katrina changed our simple notion of the city sitting on high and low ground. The storm showed that New Orleans stability is based not on high ground, but floating on a soggy humid urban landscape surrounded by a giant Mississippi River delta landscape that requires constant gardening. Change on the river is a daily routine. The silt, mud and water that pour through the subsurface soils, underground streams, bayous, drainage canals, along street curbs, down roof gutters or in the main channel of the Mississippi River are all part of the same gigantic watershed draining from 40% of the country's.

I have traveled the length of the river, from its mouth at Pilot Town, Louisiana, to its celebrated northern source at Lake Itasca, Minnesota. It is an artificial landscape or terrain from top to bottom. It is a testament to human ingenuity, spiritual quests and the creative engagement with natural processes. Katrina showed that the ground upon which the city operates is a dynamic ecological wet sponge whose ground level is affected by subsurface soil, distant deltaic wetland stability and urban tree canopy, and how streets, homes and businesses operate.

In the storm, the city lost over half of its live oaks and most of its magnolia trees, either destroyed by high winds or salt-water intrusion. The city has lost a great portion of its benevolent, symbolic and sizable urban "green canopy." Half of the City's infrastructure to reflect the heat of summer sunlight and canopy to govern the flow of constant rainfall has been lost and few are talking about the strategic importance of replacing this fundamental system, though many are thrilled about growing "green roofs" on top of new buildings. But New Orleans is not alone – in the last 25 years, Washington, D.C., has lost over 60% of its tree canopy, exposing city residents to increased heat, storm-water flooding and neighborhood decline. Meanwhile, community groups in Sacramento, California, have begun an aggressive campaign for a citywide "infrastructure" project to add thousands of trees on public and private property to enhance the city's skyline as a method to reduce living costs for families and produce a more amenable economic environment.

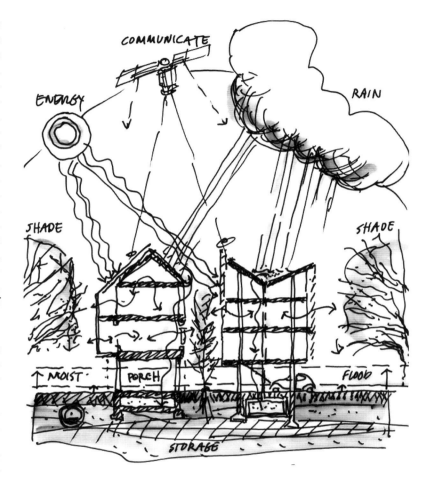

SN

Second Nature

Big and powerful natural and social ecologies have converged on this location of the lower Mississippi River to form this remarkable and unique city called New Orleans, Louisiana. The events of August 29, 2005 revealed that this city protected by the benevolent green canopy of majestic live oak trees and magnolias was a dying economic and ecological environment. The recovery requires that the city's basic natural and social ecologies reinvent a new partnership; a green hybrid landscape that is a richer mix and safer cultural soil and productive systems to generate the environment that is attractive to investment and promulgates protective regeneration.

SN   e   SN   e

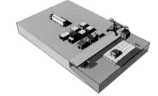

Building Blocks

The house is still largely constructed from the bottom-up by a few workers who perform many different tasks. This method requires skilled workers, controlled building sites, readily available materials, and disposal construction waste, all things that New Orleans cannot provide. Pre-fabrication offers an ideal response to NOLA's building needs. Complex construction tasks can be handled outside NOLA under ideal conditions. Delivery proceeds efficiently taking advantage of the natural flow of the Mississippi River. These barges are constructed of hollow concrete cubes and designed for one-way travel. Once arriving on site, cubes can be used in flood prone areas to provide necessary elevation on which to build. Furthermore, the hollow cubes can be used for rainwater harvesting, thermal mass, and emergency storage of water or waste. Final assembly of prefabricated elements takes place upon these block foundations. With few skills required and minimal construction waste generated, residents and neighbors can quickly assemble and inhabit each house.

e   **Building Blocks**   SN   e   SN

SN | SN |

Category 5 American City

In 2012, NOLA will celebrate its 200th anniversary as thousands of tourists from around the world inundate the city. While tourists flood by the millions through the French Quarter, NOLA is much less known for her recent history as an American City. As part of an extensive NOLA 2012 plan, outdoor recreational space and major public facilities such as museums, colleges, opera houses, and libraries will establish the land around NOLA's pumping stations as civic terrain. By building in a manner which anticipates and celebrates NOLA sogginess, NOLA will brand it's lakefront as a quintessentially American place. During the 2012 NOLA celebration, these everyday civic buildings will transform themselves into parade floats for celebratory activities. The celebration of these supposedly ordinary structures will provide the impetus for NOLA's reentry onto the global cultural scene, but no longer as the representation of colonial French culture but as the poster child for a long-lasting American tradition of risk-taking through problem solving.

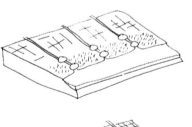

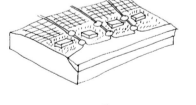

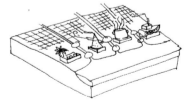

| SN | **Category 5 American City** SN

Several months later, at the other end of town, business leaders speaking on national radio interviews stated that they hadn't seen the economy this small and segregated between the wealthy and low-income workers since 1963.

A disaster like Katrina scars the existing city, leaving behind historic markings in its economic and ecological landscape. The storm coupled with the collapse of the city's basic economic and ecological system has challenged the viability of its major landmark institutions, and the norms of everyday living and working lifestyles.

In New Orleans, the everyday economic and ecological lifestyle is epitomized by the city's nickname, "The Big Easy". The economic symbol was a Mardi Gras party in the French Quarter. New Orleans received its name the Big Easy, from migrating musicians arriving from around the country and world looking for music gigs and engagement with the great New Orleans talents of the early 1900s such as Louis Armstrong. It was easy to get a job and jam with the best. Today, the Big Easy is a brand logo laminated onto a tourist t-shirt. New music and recipes are being brewed in other more cosmopolitan economies, not in the giant service kitchens of local New Orleans hotel casinos.

Once a diversified economy based on energy, finance and global trade, the city before Katrina had been reduced to a monoculture tied to tourism and entertainment. Shipping and refining had moved upriver to major barge terminals. The once industrious waterfront has become sites for wealthy condos, and/or entertainment venues for tourists. Restaurant and bars were losing qualified chefs and musicians, who moved to safer and more tolerant cosmopolitan cities.

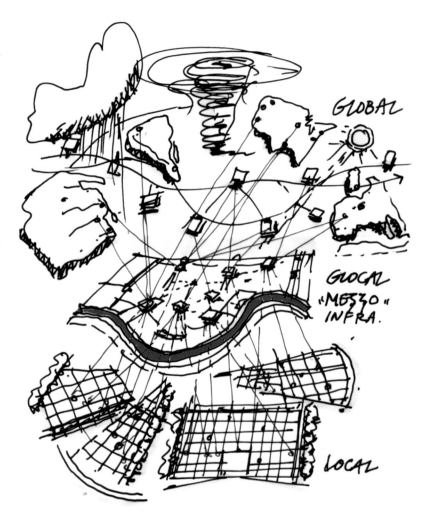

GN

Glocal Networks

New Orleans has been a global city throughout its life – once a part of France and Spain and now the United States. It is not a big city population wise, but it has produced a cultural legacy of cultural infusion in music, food and architecture known throughout the world. The storm and flood has reduced the city's population in half and it is no longer the largest city in Louisiana. Baton Rouge, the State's capital, is now larger in population. As the city rebuilds, how does it reach out to reconnect and reposition itself in the local, national and global world?

GN ∫ GN ∫

Intersecting/Absorbing: neighborhoods/ river/systéme arpent

"When the tree fell, 'it felt like an earthquake,' said Edgar Lee Smith, who rode out Katrina in his house yards away. When the storm subsided and he walked outside, 'I saw a sight I'd never seen before,' said Smith, an artist. It was the top of the old brick school building, half a block away. For the 36 years he had lived there, the building had been hidden by the giant tree's top. In all those years, his patch of Camp Street had been under a giant canopy. Now, it is sun-struck, and a bewildered magnolia is blooming." ~2006 MSN.com

Left with the radiating structure of its road system, and reintroduced to the tenuous nature the Mississippi River—Gulf Coast interface, New Orleans has little option but to embrace its precarious position. An intersecting layer can mediate the relationship between rigid and dynamic systems by permeating through both. Trees act as a meso level affecting the spatial environment at eye level, but also penetrating into the ground and the sky. This system would connect across the extent of neighborhoods in New Orleans, filling in the spaces that fallen oaks have left behind and making a new statement about who these trees are for. This system would be absorbed into the greater networking of the city, and would also absorb the shock (both physical and psychological) of shifts in natural systems. The word 'catastrophe' would soon become obsolete.

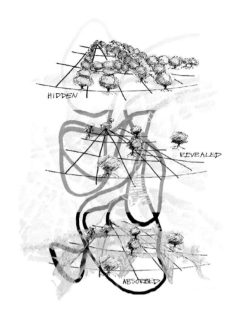

∫ GN ∫ Intersecting/Absorbing GN

GN ℮ GN ℮

Supply-shed

The modular production supply chain of the automobile industry is adapted here to fit the immediate house and long-term economic needs of New Orleans. A watershed of parts, the headwaters are tier 2 suppliers who may only produce a single part for delivery to tier 1.5 suppliers. The tier 1.5 supplier creates systems to the specifications of a tier 1 supplier. The tier 1 supplier is responsible for constructing larger modules containing many systems. These self-supporting modules are delivered to the assembler, who bolts together the modules to form the final product. At each level suppliers are only responsible for a limited number of tasks, allowing them produce quality products and have confidence in their supplies. In a modular production chain for New Orleans housing, tier 2 and 1.5 subassemblies may be located across the country. Tier 1 suppliers are located closer to or in the city, limiting the delivery challenges posed by larger elements. Final assembly can take place on each in neighborhoods or at strategic sites around the city. This chain would continue to supply houses to the Gulf Coast until demand drops, then reorient itself to production and delivery of survivable modular homes to disaster struck areas in the US, Caribbean, and Latin America.

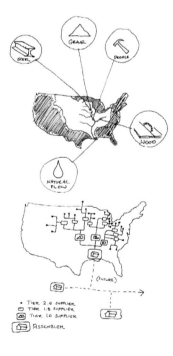

℮ Supply-shed GN ℮ GN

We take for granted that our cities are rooted on solid economic foundations and supported by a benevolent environment. In fact, cities float upon dynamic economic and ecological processes.

Cities which neglect the maintenance and upgrade of their basic economic and ecological footings are left to radical and swift change due to weather events such as Katrina. Cities are constantly changing, typically at a slower rate that allows for a city to make certain decisions to amend upward and downward growth trends. New Orleans now faces major economic and ecological generational change on all fronts with little time, faltering infrastructure, half of its population, and a weak tax base.

New Orleans' precarious situation should not be ignored by other American cities, thinking that they live far away from hurricanes and harm's way. Los Angeles sits on massive earthquake faults and at the end of long-distance water lines to support basic survival. Atlanta, Georgia is perched on stone with little ability to store the water necessary for a growing city. Each city shapes its economics and ecological circumstance to form what J. B. Jackson describes as a pair of ideal landscapes, the political landscape – or collective community and inhabited landscape – or everyday citizen realm. The quality of a citiy's life is rooted in its making its basic values of health, safety and welfare vivid in its infrastructure. Typically built out of sight, J.B. Jackson reminds us that this artificial landscape or terrain is sustained and constructed of levees, canals, water treatment plants, pumps, power stations parks, police stations, schools, and other systems to form the governing background to the city's political landscape and public realm.

The first half of the ideal landscape is united with the second half, the inhabited landscape. This is the everyday or quotidian landscape of homes, gardens, neighborhoods operating not as a giant isolated land use at the end of utility service lines, but as a field of fine domestic infrastructure networks working to reduce external costs, generate the energy to support the local economy and resources for a fertile ecology. Uniting these two worlds in support of each other is at the heart of what it means to be a cosmopolitan city and is the baseline for resetting the City of New Orleans next "high ground".

New Orleans will be 300 years old in 2018. Our nation should turn its great commonwealth of ingenuity, creativity and energy towards New Orleans. New Orleans needs to open its doors to more transparent, inclusive and tolerant governance. Together, we can learn to rebuild one of our nation's first international cities (founded in 1718) into a world center for taking risks to create the next generation of cosmopolitan community -- a "global gumbo city" filled with a mélange of entrepreneurial ideas welling up from cultural diversity and anchored in the ecological roux of Mississippi River basins.

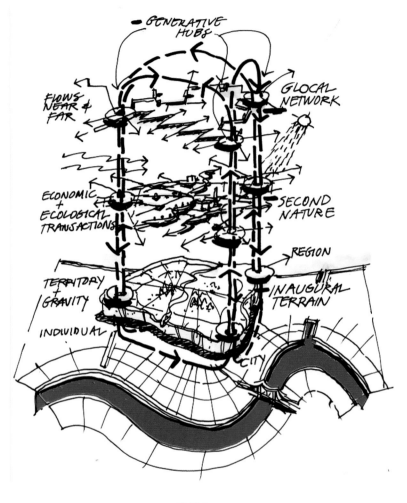

GH

Generative Hubs

Before Katrina, the historic French quarter, neighborhood corner jazz joints and cafes, and the giant drainage pumps were the primary cultural hubs of economic and ecological sustainability. The events of 29 August revealed that they were fading stars in the urban landscape. Musicians were leaving, the downtown economy was in trouble, and the pumps and canals were inadequate. These are still important pivot points for recovery, but the activities of rebuilding are creating potentially new hubs of cultural activity that will frame the civic infrastructure of the city's future.

GH e GH e

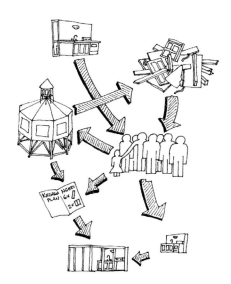

Engaged Ad hoc

In Katrina's aftermath many have called for a massive government rebuilding effort. The scale of this effort is measured in hundreds of thousands of trailers, millions of acres of flooded land, and billions of dollars. Amidst this scale, it may be tempting to dismiss the ad-hoc as too complicated or ineffective. But, the ad-hoc has the potential to transcend and engage. In WWII, the Victory Garden campaign urged families to plant their own vegetable gardens to supply them with food and reduce demand for canned goods bound for troops overseas. At its peak, the program sprouted 20 million gardens and produced 40 percent of all vegetables grown in the U.S. A grassroots effort to encourage the ad-hoc repair and production of homes could prove immensely beneficial to New Orleans and the Gulf Coast. Proposed is a hybrid construction system which splits intensive and extensive tasks. Intensive processes would create self-supporting modules using skilled labor and specialized facilities. These modules would be delivered to residents who complete the extensive tasks. Once on site, residents would extend the prefabricated modules with salvaged materials to form a structure. Community lighthouses would provide design guidelines on how to construct structures and arrange for the collection and distribution of appropriate salvaged materials.

e **Engaged Ad hoc** GH e GH

GH f GH f

Shifting/Success-ing: pioneers under altered conditions

The drastic change in environmental conditions of the city has triggered a process of urban succession, as well an opportunity to guide succession in a new way. In the phases of this successional city, a forest grows and diversifies itself, creating optimal conditions for those communities that have been devalued. It becomes a slow process of colonizing the disturbed environment. Immediate canopy cover and water absorption supplied by trees provide the desire and the 'shelter' for urban infill—density of settlement is contingent on density of vegetation. Species of vegetation is also a contributor to identity whether at the scale of the street, neighborhood, or city. These unique subsystems begin to cross over into other territories as the urban forest grows, connecting neighborhoods and growing into the larger identity of the city.

The city was founded on a structure that was valued from the outside inward; the future is to value from the inside out.

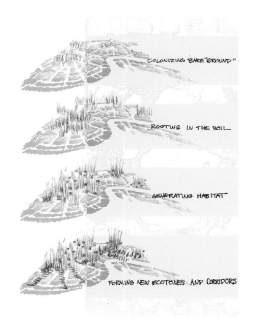

COLONIZING BARE "GROUND"

ROOTING IN THE SOIL

GENERATING HABITAT

FORMING NEW ECOTONES AND CORRIDORS

f GH f **Shifting/Success-ing** GH

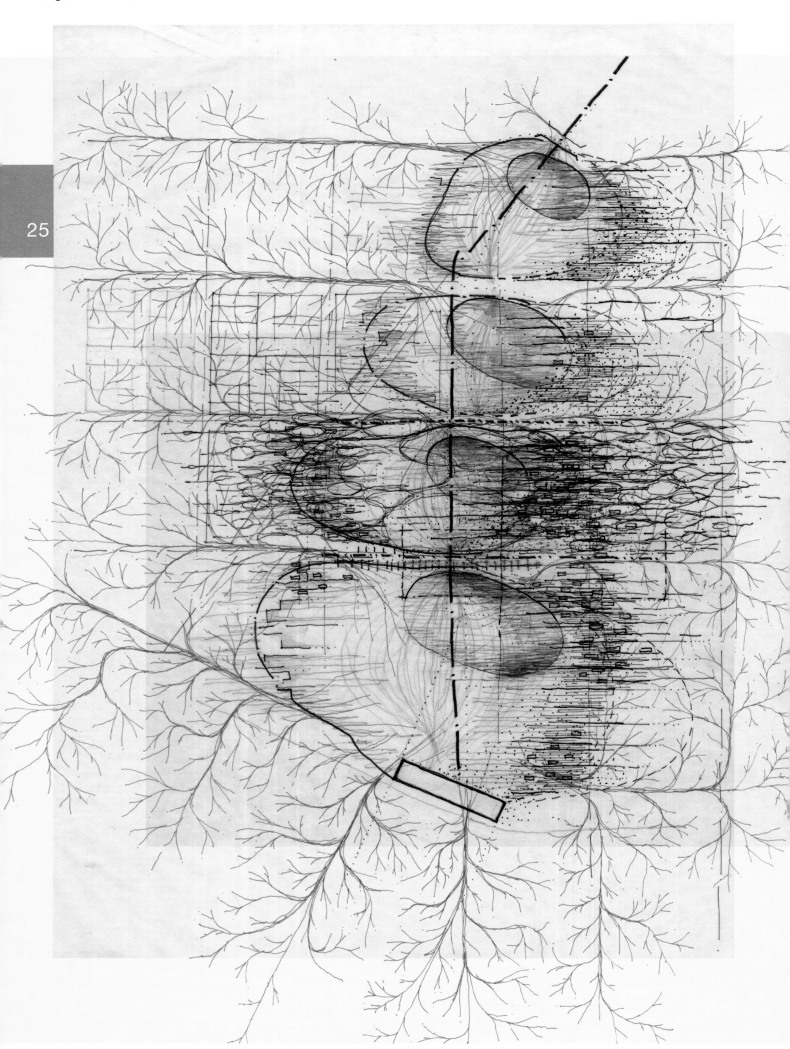

The founding of New Orleans might very well have been a bad idea. Within almost all contemporary urban models for understanding a city, the wild, yet fragile natural setting of the lower Mississippi has shown time and time again how inhospitable a place this is. And yet it is this very condition that has attracted so many poets, musicians, picarunes, and visionaries to settle here. But as the numbers increased, that original roguish place at the margins has become a rather conventional example of human engineering designed to tame and erase the natural processes that gave the area such a strong aura in the first place.

Now, once again, New Orleans has to confront what it is. The options are few: It can be abandoned for a new start on higher ground, or it can be rebuilt with massive but mostly short-lived protections against further acts of nature with the outcome of nature being pushed even further from human consciousness. Neither of these options seems attractive.

This studio has explored a different strategy. Early histories of the lower Mississippi gave a vivid picture of the inventive ways that hunters, trappers, and others co-existed with the swamps and bayous in a mutually supportive existence. Our working assumption is that this same attitude can prove instructive for re-inhabiting areas of the city that otherwise would not prove viable.

The studio found much evidence of cultures that have been built effectively on water. In all cases, the engagement of natural process with culture produced a reciprocity where the flows and energies of nature were accepted and therefore accommodated. This extended even to methods of agriculture and the harvesting of fish as part of a more sustainable approach to urban infrastructure.

The question of permanence in such a dynamic set of natural forces had to be revisited. This will influence the choice of material systems, methods of construction, as well as the relationship between the individual and the community. Is heroic resistance to extreme conditions the most effective safeguard or might one imagine a more ephemeral construction capable of rapid and simple rebuilding? And within a city already unable to adequately maintain its public infrastructure, might there be ways that the reconstituted private realm assume more responsibility for its infrastructural needs? In other words, how would it be possible to maintain the idea of New Orleans but under more sustainable conditions?

The study area was the Broadmoor neighborhood. Broadmoor is at the center of New Orleans and is a place where major street systems, drainage systems, and other parts of the urban infrastructure converge. Since it is mostly a bowl sitting below sea level, it also is where vast quantities of water converge. It was settled mostly since the 1920's before which it was a productive swamp. Its urbanization went against previous practices of not building in the backwaters. While some have suggested that the area should not be re-inhabited, to us this would have meant ripping out the very heart of the city. Instead, what is illustrated here are proposals that demonstrate how the no longer acknowledged underlying wetness of the place can become the foundation for a more vital, sustainable community.

left: site drainage watershed and flow
right: wetland micropools and relation-
ship to exisiting city fabric
site digram drawings by Jim Richardson

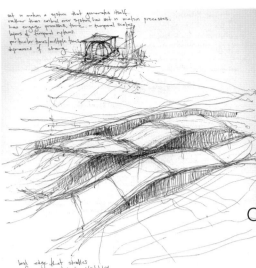

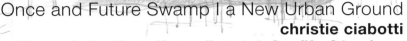

christie ciabotti

Disastrous flooding following Hurricane Katrina in the City of New Orleans demonstrated a fundamental opposition in the urban structure between the dynamic forces of water surrounding the crescent city and the people who seek always to control and manipulate these forces. My study proposes a more flexible and absorptive way of living on soggy ground that seeks to harmonize the relationship of man and nature while retaining a dense urban context. Focusing on the neighborhood of Broadmoor, one of the lowest points in the city and one of the most central points in the city, I propose a return to the watery cypress backswamp landscape that caused this part of the city to be one of the latest developed.

The existing geometry of the street grid in Broadmoor, which was greatly influenced by the French arpent system, integrally connects the neighborhood to the river through the city. Picking up on these urban geometries, the project seeks to maintain the density and structure of the area while building a light and flexible raised ground of bicycle and pedestrian ways that integrates with the watery ground of swamp and vertical elements of cypress trees. Raised houses along these "streets" are constructed to cultivate public life with front porches, creating a gradient from the public street to the private core of the house. Each house is integrated into the swamp landscape and ecosystem and into the urban systems of city street-like and civic infrastructures.

A swamp, characterized by low gradient, muddy bottom channels and silty brackish water, has the potential in this area to mitigate the effects of flooding that occur often in Broadmoor – soaking rain and thunderstorms cause routine flooding here. This proposal suggests a reshaping of the ground plane in Broadmoor to create depressions in an already low area to support an "infrastructure" of cypress swamp ecosystem that would in turn support a new kind of absorptive urban form. In this way, a set of new grounds, responsive and flexible, would start to develop in the City of New Orleans. The primary canopy species, Taxodium distichum of Bald Cypress, defines the vertical form of the swamp.

above: Initial sketch exploring topographical opportunities to initiate a structure of habitation

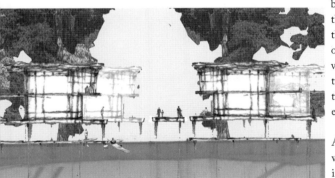

Structures occupy the wet lowlands in similar manner to the fishing camps, replicating the natural dynamic of the bayou.

right: Using construction techniques related more to marine environments acknowledges the inevitable presence of water. A new elevated public ground engages the wet, soggy ground below revealing a richly diverse ecology that now is able to be revalued and celebrated as a part of public consciousness.

left study models: The Broadmoor grid showing the arpent structure of streets linking the Mississippi to the backwater area, although typically described as a bowl, a more fine grain analysis of the topography of Broadmoor reveals a more complex gradation from wet to dry, and the topography defines a subset of distinct areas within the larger neighborhood.

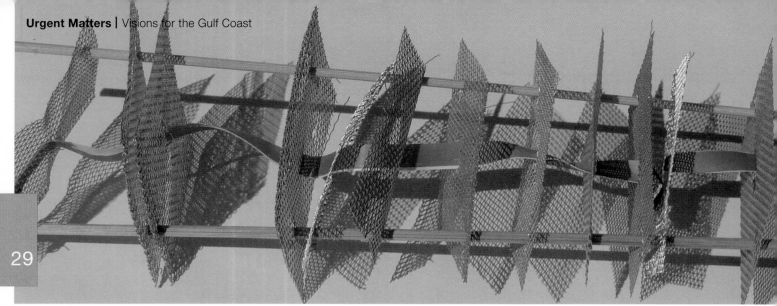

Initial thoughts in this study model show hydrological-cal flows more easily engaging urban structure.

right: New Orleans collage model showing canals, arpents, and topography

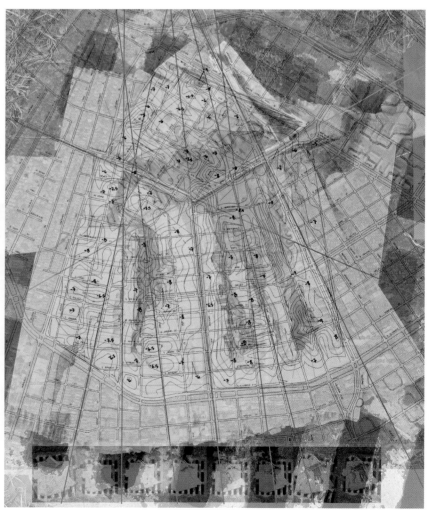

diagram base-plan drawing with street grid and 6 inch contour lines showing flood depths

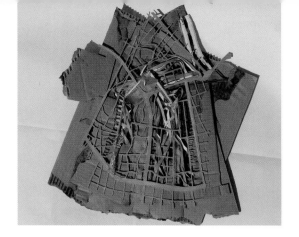

cession I return I restore
PROgression I re-cycle I re-place
beth kaleida

This study was initially inspired by the microtopography of New Orleans, the condition of inundation, sedimentation, subsidence, and filtration that occurred in the swamp and bayou that formerly existed in Broadmoor area. My first efforts were to find information about the topography of the area. Due to the changeability of the ground, the minimal grade, and perhaps organizational and bureaucratic issues, one foot topological information is not publicly made available for this region where four feet may make a difference between devastation and survival – low and wet to high and dry.

My initial studies looked at the existing systems of topography, political boundaries (arpent lines), and urban infrastructure (drainage canals). A sketch model made suggestions for a redivisioning and regarding of the site to allow for more diversity of degrees of flooding and visual manifestation of rising water.

Re-envisioning the relationship between earth, water and house in the Broadmoor neighborhood of New Orleans became the focus of my design problem. In order to heighten awareness of the presence and fluctuation of water as well as serve as a neighborhood and city amenity, water flows through the neighborhood in a passive stormwater control system of marsh, lake, and swamp. The pumps and underground canals of New Orleans become the secondary system.

A linear park path follows the path of the water through the neighborhood, increasing interaction with water. The west side of the neighborhood is the highest, and water here is directed into a marsh where grasses begin to remove heavy metals and lead from the stormwater. A system of gabion walls and pocket parks lines the west edge of the park and marks the route of a former road that extends from historic apent boundaries. The path becomes elevated as it crosses over the road, and opens onto the second story back terraces to a high water level adjacent to a lake where sediment drops out of water as it moves toward the east.

A model wasa flooded with a suspension of coffee grounds in water in order to envision the process of the flood and observe sediment movement. This base was later built upon as a study model.

A new system of wet urban parks establishes new neighborhood patterns.

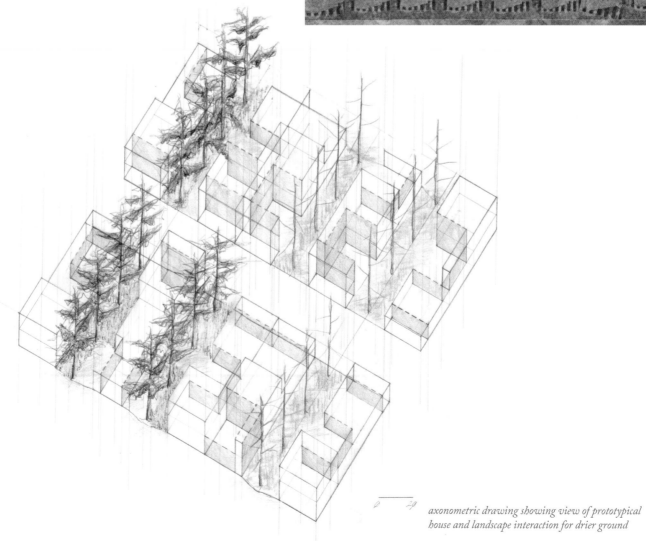

axonometric drawing showing view of prototypical house and landscape interaction for drier ground

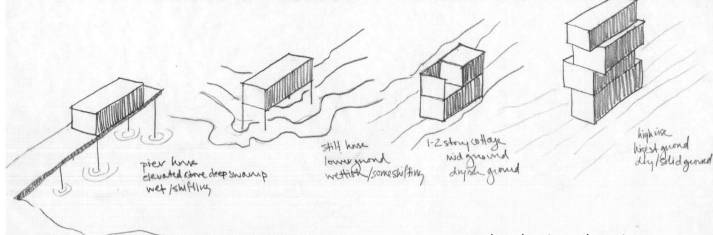

housing type sketches relative to the wetness of the ground

Water can exit and enter the neighborhood system via the pumphouse in order to manage water levels in times of drought or flood. From the lake, water is directed into a series of stepped stormwater filtration pools adjacent to another line of commercial buildings with outdoor terraces. The pools vary in depth and material, and serve to filter, aerate, and purify water before it enters the main area of swamp in the east side of the site. Grasses and cypress trees remove heavy metals and lead, and other pollutants through a system of phyto-remediation. The varying surfaces of sheeting area activate water in order to modify sounds and reflection. Water passes under Broad Street and into habitable cypress swamps, which is stocked with crawfish and open for public recreation, fishing, and boating. Private boat slips line the adjacent neighborhood streets.

The park culminates in a series of long, thin piers reaching out into the deep-water swamp. A return pipe here controls overflow by returning water to the neighborhood lake or to the pumphouse in times of flooding. Water that leaves the system has been purified, and thus does not contribute to the pollution of Lake Pontchartrain.

above: A new filtration plant along with much-needed new commercial facilities form a public place that celebrates a hybrid system of water management. The stepped and ramped surfaces become the means by which the fluctuations in water level are measured and made part of public life.

left: site model

*Instead of the heroically flawed attempts to control nature
with levees, here water is let into the neighborhood and
spread out over a large area. Earthworks, foundations, terracing, and other topographical interventions
necessary for building the new housing structure are
leveraged to direct the now lower velocities of flooding
into a hybrid ecological structure of swales, bio retention
ponds, and dispersed networks of pumping stations
that is the basis for a new form of inhabited garden.*

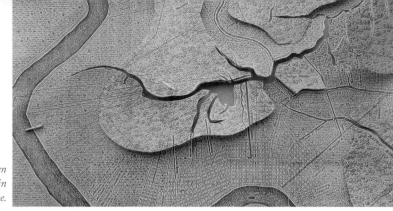

Pattern of ridges and bayous that were hidden
by the overlaid political grid can once again
form the basis of an inhabited landscape.

Constructing Ground | Growing Environments
The Dynamic House and Garden of New Orleans
anne bohlen

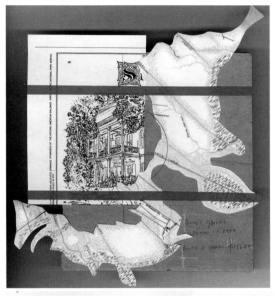

This thesis proposes that the process of rebuilding in New Orleans is not simply a process of repeating what has failed but rather that this rebuilding should foremost be a time of reconsidering the community's reliance upon its infrastructure and questions how the infrastructure can become embedded in the relationship between house and garden. Instead of viewing infrastructure as a one-sided, non-systematic series of levees, the question became how to embed the infrastructure into the life of the city in a manner which strives to create environments which can function and evolve into dynamic, flexible ecosystems.

The focus of this project therefore was to examine closely the smaller scale instances of the urban environment, expanding their own definitions and attempting to make them part of a holistic infrastructural environment while establishing new parameters for the idea of community and neighborhood. Out of this came my thesis: What is the relationship of the house to the ground in New Orleans and how can this relationship be reinvented in a manner consistent with the infrastructural needs of the city?

I began to investigate the idea of the walls of the house and more specifically the foundation. Intrigued by vertical garden installation of Patrick Blanc, as well as speculative projects such as BioLung, the foundation of the house began to take on a life of its own as I started to design a vertical wetland within the frame of the foundation. In this manner, the house starts to act as a living unit within the infrastructure able to capture and direct the flow of water. It slows, cleanses, and releases water into a set of pools adjacent to the house which encompasses the garden of the home. These pooling areas act as public courtyards and areas of occupation, activating the interior of the blocks and pulling the public realm into the living infrastructure. Each home acts as its own insulation with the capacity to absorb rising water levels. Surrounding the houses is a larger scale infrastructural environment, which receives water from the houses and eventually grows into a healthy eco-system.

The porch seen as part of the garden as well as part of the house becomes the metaphor and the means by which the neighborhood can be rebuilt to work with the natural flows that previously have been ignored. Initial sketches show the potential relationships between houses, water, and tree cover.

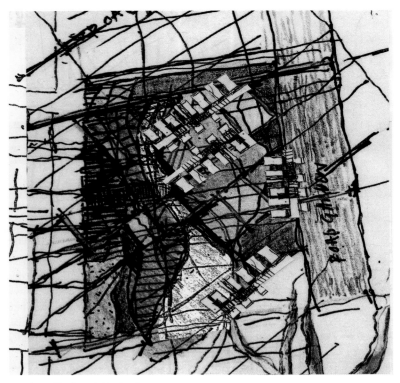

early studies for neighborhood structure.

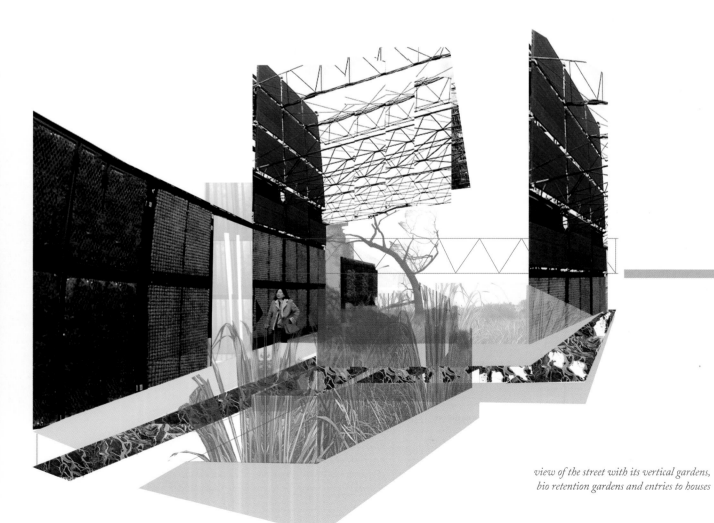

*view of the street with its vertical gardens,
bio retention gardens and entries to houses*

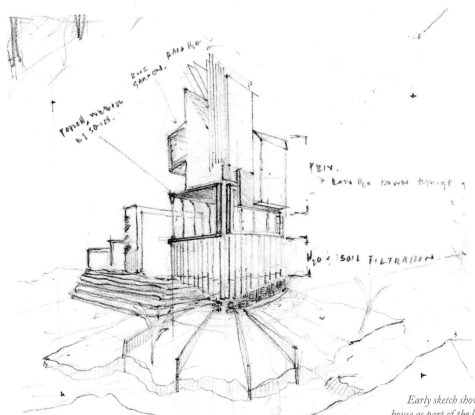

Constructing Ground | Growing Environments
The Dynamic House and Garden of New Orleans

anne bohlen

Early diagrams and models explored how the process of growing this environment would occur. Layers of infrastructure relating to the pumping station would be built first, this would then be followed by layers of debris such aa fallen trees to initiate an organic layer; houses would then be built activating the system. The foundations would control the flow of water and begin to establish 'natural' stream corridors throughout the gardens and into the larger swale system. In this way, the landscape begins to grow as a living infrastructural system only through the relationship of the house and ground.

The site where I chose to implement this strategy is within the lowest area of the neighborhood of Broadmoor. A topographic bathtub, it lies in approximate adjacency to the number 1 pumping station in Broadmoor. This decision developed an infrastructural environment which would be able to maintain an overflow amount of water during times of emergency while water levels could simultaneously be maintained during safe times by the pumping station. In this respect, the relationship between the house, garden and pumping station is envisioned as a "symbiotic machine in the garden".

Early sketch showing the foundation of the house as part of the larger topography directing the flows of groundwater with the house itself collecting, storing, and distributing rainwater.

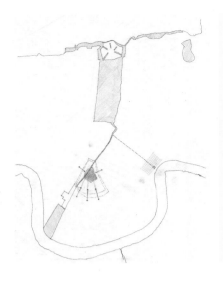
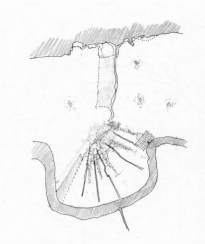
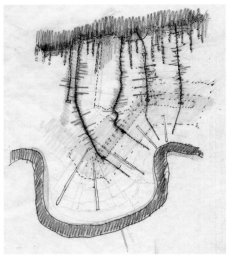

above: These diagrams describe the relationship of the Broadmoor neighborhood to New Orleans. Diagram #1 shows the neighborhood's connection to significant parks and how the neighborhood could link these together to create a transect from the Mississippi to Lake Pontchartrain. Diagram #2: The new lake and swamp are a result of restoring the topography and processes that would have created the original lake and swamp before development suppressed these. Diagram #3 shows the creation of new bayous along existing canals to help reduce the dramatic influxes of water, as well as creating new flood zones. These bayous would tie into the city's water pump system, to allow for circulation of water, resulting in a new hybrid ecosystem.

The Broadmoor neighborhood now ties into the existing infrastructure and topography of New Orleans. Located at the base of New Orleans, it is also a location where many of the historic plantations drained their water.

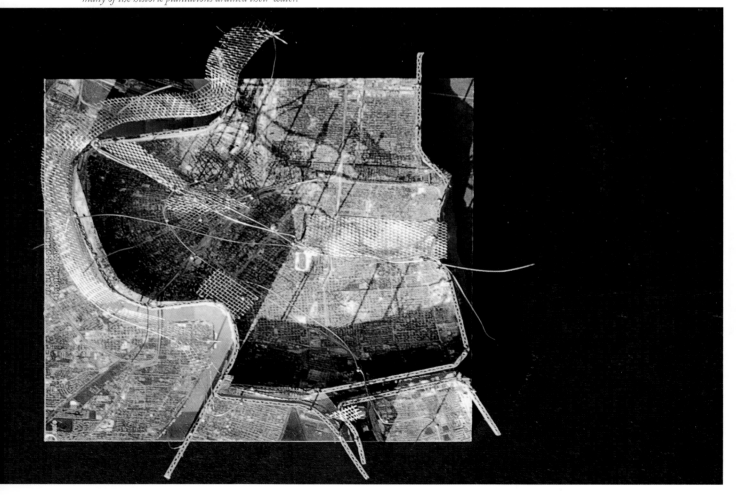

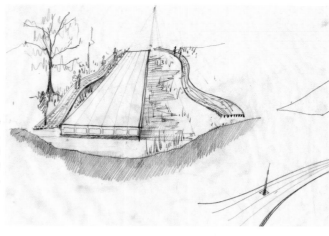

Roads are constructed to float during high water becoming places of safety in flood conditions. The pedestrian walkways would be separated from the road so that people could weave through the bayou infrastructure to understand New Orleans' unique environment.

This project works to connect built structures to natural systems. Because Broadmoor is at the bottom of the bowl of New Orleans, it is wetter than other parts of the city. In fact, a lake was once located here. However, this system of water collection has been erased by a series of drainage canals. This design works to reveal this water collection and celebrate it. It assumes that the levees will be rebuilt to what they were pre-Katrina.

Originally, New Orleans dealt with the swamp by keeping the city small. However, as the population increased, the city spread into the wetter parts of the landscape. In 1949, Broadmoor was developed; at this time, most houses were built slab on grade, creating an unsafe environment for future flooding. This was resolved with high dependence on the drainage canal system. Unfortunately, disasters such as Katrina proved that the canal system is no longer dependable.

It is vital for the people of New Orleans to be able to see the ecosystems working around them in order to understand how the water will flow and to have a stronger connection to shifting water levels. Living with the natural systems will enrich the New Orleans culture that still maintains it as part of its past.

Currently, Broadmoor's topography does not work with the street structure. This results in a difficult evacuation of people and water. Furthermore, the public places of Broadmoor are dispersed and most are outside of the neighborhood. The design here proposes a more connective topography. By using the existing topography and making cuts strategically, water is allowed to flow. This is also aided by the construction of weirs, which help drain the higher areas of the neighborhood, but also retain the water in the lower areas to allow infiltration back to the water table. It is essential for the weirs to direct water so that primary North/South streets will remain dry if evacuations become necessary. Finally, there are zones between higher and lower ground, which become places for collection for people, materials, water, and soil. Therefore, these high and low areas of Broadmoor are to take on different characteristics. The higher parts of the neighborhood will have a higher density than those in the lower parts, as shown in figure 6. Between these spaces is a collection zone that will function as a community gathering place.

Through this process of gradually re-occupying the land, people of Broadmoor will be able to enjoy the benefits of working with the natural systems. Here the wet helps to create an identity and a greater understanding of the ecosystem.

A bayou works as part of the infrastructure to assist in slowing down the water. Weirs will also slow down flood waters and, at the same time, become supports for other structures-in this case a pedestrian walkway. This walkway has the potential of educating individuals about the identity of their place and methods of building within it.

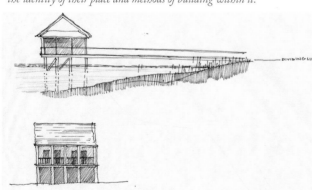

Two traditional New Orleans houses. The top is for wetland and is built on stilts out in the water. This house type allows for easy rebuilding on the existing stilt structure in case of severe storm. The one below shows a house for a drier area and has a first floor of stone that would keep the house safe in case of flooding.

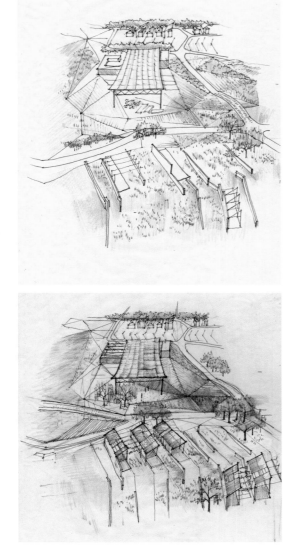

These images illustrate the process of reconstruction. It begins with an understanding of the existing conditions and the results of flooding after hurricane Katrina. Afterwards, a number of houses are taken down after analyzing different criteria to determine their safety: the height of the topography, the year the house was built (earlier is better), and the number of stories. This will result in several houses along Napoleon remaining but most along Louisiana Avenue being taken down. The materials of the houses will be gathered and sorted at the collection zone. Materials that can be reused will be recycled as building materials for houses in the higher parts of the neighborhood. In the meantime, the low areas will go through a process of soil remediation to clear out many of the toxins in the existing soil. Soils with very high toxicity will be removed to other collection zones for extensive remediation.

During this time, weirs will begin to be constructed to help direct the flow of water to the lower areas. Gradually, the higher areas will become denser, and when the soil reaches safe levels, the lower areas will become places for agriculture. This will require the water to be filtered before it enters this lower part of the site, at the edge of the collection zone. Eventually, small houses could be constructed in this area to harvest the crawfish, rice, and soybeans produced here. Finally, at this stage, the collection zone becomes a farmers market for the exchange of food.

below: Places of wet are constructed with weirs to help direct and slow the movement of water, allowing sediment to be discharged. The resultant wet places work as a sponge to balance extremes in water flow. This process creates high ground for increased housing density and provides dry routes for safe evacuation. Between the places of dry and places of wet would be a series of community spaces for collection of people, building materials, and markets.

 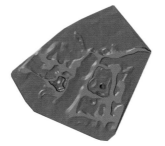  

*above: Modeling the microtopography
reveals the structure of water flows.*

41

*The infrastructure of the house operates as an
extension of the bayou ecological process.*

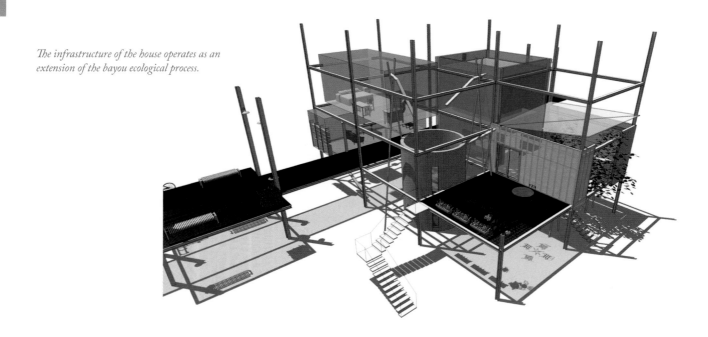

*below: Image shows the swamp landscape reconfigured
and managed as part of the social-cultural infrastructure.*

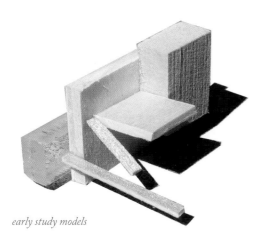

early study models

Creating an Urban Backyard Bayou

christina kang

In considering a rebuilding project in New Orleans, it is impossible to examine the effects of Hurricane Katrina without an investigation into the infrastructure of the city. Short- and long-term building strategies are dependent upon a greater system that will provide order and stability for the present, and one that will consider safety and welfare in the vulnerable city in the years to come.

life in the Backyard Bayou.

Because of my initial interest in the infrastructural systems of the city, I became aware on our trip of several instances of "heroic infrastructure" - the levees that were designed to single-handedly protect the city, the major highways (i.e., I-10) soaring over once-thriving commercial and social spaces, a major pumping station designed to serve several neighborhoods without fail. These examples of city infrastructure were built with little regard for the dynamic landscape of the specific place and for the social networks that were springing up naturally within it. The rebuilding of New Orleans calls for a more flexible, mediating relationship between the nature of the land and the necessity of the infrastructure.

For most, the first task is to rebuild homes for displaced residents. However, without a system to build upon, the danger of returning to the same vulnerable state before the storm is imminent. This project seeks to create a better dialogue between the natural dynamic processes of the particular place of New Orleans and the new rebuilt form. With a better mediating system, both can live simultaneously, with one not taking anything away from the other, and the urban identity of the community can also be preserved within a new kind of living.

After an initial investigation into some of the larger infrastructural systems of the city, the project focus shifted to the neighborhood of Broadmoor, located Uptown, at one of the lowest elevations of the city. Two issues came to the forefront - the heroic systems that included no redundancies in case of failure and the dynamic nature of the land.

The first step in the process of reconceiving this place was to bring the water back in. With topographical changes, water can flow in a controlled manner through the neighborhood with smaller pumps directing flow and allowing for flooding if necessary. The ground then becomes wet in places, dry in places, and in-between in others, depending on flood and rain conditions. Dwellings would face onto the newly-formed wetlands, to create a "backyard bayou" condition that recalls elements of a prior condition of living while also maintaining a unique urban identity.

A series of smaller interventions layered on the new ground allows for a redundancy of systems at the scale of the neighborhood clusters. The neighborhood itself would become mainly pedestrian, where cars could be parked on higher points near automobile entry points and could easily be evacuated in times of emergency. The walkway system becomes the new constructed ground over the naturally dynamic ground, which is allowed to move and change, flood and recede, at will. It is within this structure that housing is rebuilt, raised above the maximum flood level to provide a stable living condition. The flexible structure allows for houses approximately the size of a shotgun house or for multifamily housing for single people or smaller families. It also allows for much-needed retail and community gathering spaces for groceries, coffee shops, laundromats, etc.

43

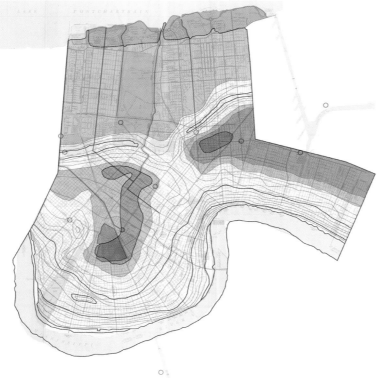

artificial terrain analysis

In the early 1900's, A.B. Wood invented the wood screw pump, a mechanical device powerful enough to drain water against gravity. The implementation of pumps, canals, and levee walls created a newly "dry" artificial terrain that allowed people to move into the wilderness. This new artificial terrain offered the benefits of a suburb in the downtown area of New Orleans, (for better or worse) supposedly eliminating the correlation of race and class with topographic advantage. These "draining machines" gave a (false) sense that the human was in control of nature. A city that respected its situation and attempted to work within its risks and rewards was replaced by slab on grade construction, tolerance to sin and a general easy-going attitude. The city engaged in a series of invasive topographic changes to keep water out, remove water, create new land, and improve navigation. An infrastructural network of pumping stations, levee walls and canals (re)organized the city below the surface of the ground.

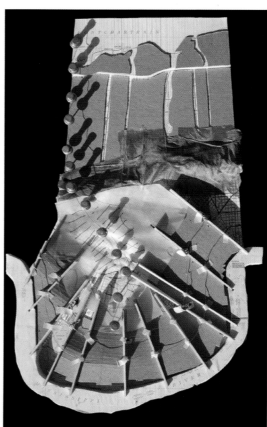

New Orleans anaylsis model

Settled on the highest ground possible, New Orleans became the crescent shape of flooded silt deposits on the inside of the natural levee. Land was organized by the French arpent system to maximize the number of plots that could access the Mississippi River as a natural resource. Narrow wedges of farmland traced the river's edge and stretched toward the back swamp.

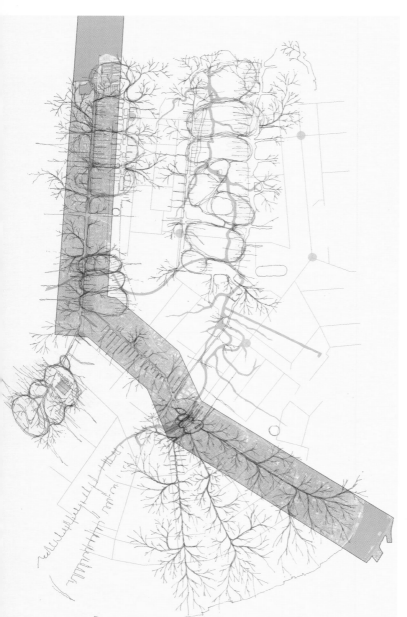

city diagram of the 17th Street canal and watershed

aerial site photograph: culmination of 17th street canal at pumping station number 1

bird's eye perspective: open air canal and pumping station number 1

My project recognizes pumping station number 1 and its adjacent open air canal as the city low point. The pumping station is at the geometric center of New Orleans, a topographic bowl, a vortex where systems of infrastructure converge. It exists at an edge between the extent of the natural levee and drained land below the levels of the Mississippi River and Lake Pontchartrain. It is a neighborhood keystone bordering Gert Town to the north, B.W. Cooper Apartments to the east, Central City to the south, and Broadmoor to the west. In the 1800's, the site for the pumping station was part of a 12-acre lake that connected to Bayou St. John.

During our site visit to New Orleans, I was fascinated with the powerful space made by the concrete open air canal and the potential for the pumping station to become a center for community gathering. Surrounded by a moat of water, the pumping station sits in the middle of S. Broad Street like a prominent rock in a stream, plugged into the complex network of under street canals. It is a landmark of orientation and an amphibious terrain, constantly in flux oscillating between wet and dry. After a rain, the pumping station can pump 2.6 million gallons of water per minute toward Lake Pontchartrain. During regular operation, the canal is dry.

As a design intervention, the amphibious terrain is reconsidered as productive and possessing a unique set of values and opportunities. This proposed wetland prototype becomes an operational landscape. The concrete canal is replaced by a constructed tidal wetland and collection basin that naturally promotes infiltration, storm water collection and remediation. Crawfish flourish in the shallow marsh and rice is harvested. Periodic fluctuations in the water level become a mechanism for annual renewal of the landscape. Pockets of community gathering and dwelling form at the interstice of the block precondition and the intervention of amphibious wetland arpents.

Throughout its history, New Orleans has reinvented its relationship with its ground. Before its founding, it was a swamp, a vital and dynamic wetland frequented by rappers, fishermen, and pirates. However, its strategic situation at the mouth of the Mississippi River demanded a city; a place without a plan. Settled on the highest ground possible, New Orleans became the crescent shape of flooded silt deposits on the inside of the natural levee. Land was organized by the French arpent system to maximize the number of plots that could access the Mississippi River as a natural resource. Narrow wedges of farmland traced the river's edge and stretched toward the back swamp. Water obtained from the river was used for agriculture and then discharged to the lower lands. Arpent property boundaries became irrigation canals, stormwater channels and natural avenues for circulation. The back swamp became a place for cultural gathering.

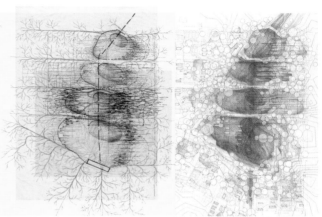

site digrams
left: site drainage watershed and flow
right: wetland micropools and relation-ship to exisiting city fabric

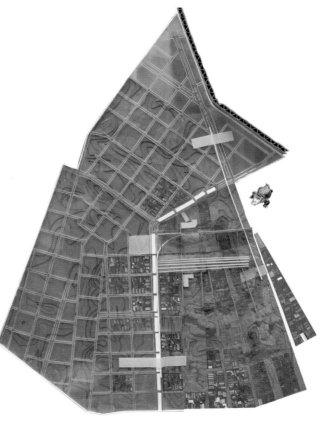

site analysis model: Broadmoor neighborhood

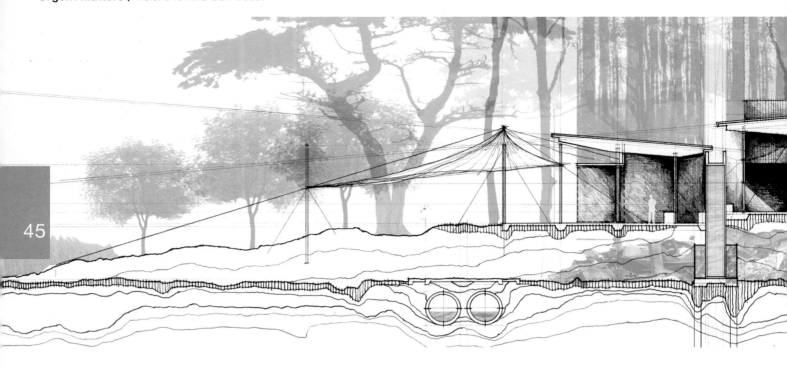

above: site plan drawing of church proposal
below: views of the site model

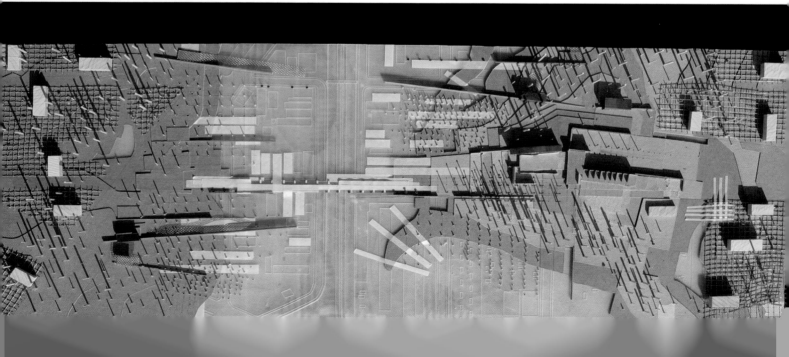

above: site section

My project proposes a church as a way for the people of New Orleans to re-imagine their city. Churches and other neighborhood-gathering institutions in New Orleans, such as schools and Social Aid Pleasure Clubs, provide the neutral ground for citizens to gather. During Hurricane Katrina, these institutions provided refuge and have continued to serve as hubs for repopulation of the city. Such centers on high ground provide means for citizens to return to the city in order to participate in the gutting and grieving process and move on with their lives. The accumulation of community events at the church provides a way station for the repopulation of the city.

At a crossing in the road, where an emergent wetland forest of cypress integrates with the existing city fabric, where gutted debris is collected, a place of everyday overlap is created. Ground tires, fallen trees and discarded refrigerators establish a new terrain against a structure of garden walls. The gabion walls act as wetland weirs, directing water between them and allowing seepage through them. Areas of shade induce gathering, and water is collected for a lightweight roof into a cistern. At once, this place is a church, a school, and a community center.

The program of the church provides for the everyday (and temporary), the occasional (and sacred), and the emergencies (catastrophe). It is first a shelter with essential services: a protective roof from the elements, dry ground on which to unfold a bunk, and an abundance of toilets, sinks, and indoor/outdoor showers with varying levels of privacy. The plan is organized about the cistern, the spine of water collection and distribution along the roof's valley. A sacristy protects valuables and becomes a library and side chapel for individual meditation. A kitchen serves the community and extends itself into a farmers market. A classroom opens into a work yard, where building materials are stored and Mardi Gras floats are constructed and stored. Dormitories house families while they learn how to rebuild their homes and lives. Within this diagram of events, a sanctuary (one good room) of versatile gathering is created to function for this neighborhood in flux.

47

RE-imagining levee
as urban infrastructure
jordan phemister

New Orleans is both predicated upon the Mississippi River for trade and transport, and reliant upon physical separation from the river and its larger hydrologic system for its day-to-day existence. I began this project by analyzing the geology, hydrology and historical mappings of New Orleans. In February 2005, our studio traveled to the city. It was an incredible experience which included biking all over, experiencing the devastation from the ground, demolishing a house and discarding its countless belongings, and an evening at Miss Doll's, a local bar filled with local people who managed to be welcoming, generous, and quick with a smile in spite of their broken hearts, houses, and neighborhoods. A critical moment during the trip for me was a failed attempt to reach the Mississippi River from Napoleon Avenue, a primary road oriented roughly north to south reflecting the historic arpent system of land division along the Mississippi River. We arrived on our bikes at a barred gate probably less than five hundred feet from the river, and the woman working the gate could not tell us how to get to the river. After further analysis, I found that nearly the entire southern sweep of the city between downtown to the east and Audubon Park to the west was occupied by port facilities, preventing public access to a significant portion of the river's edge from within the city.

This project sought to re-imagine this interface between city and river. I transformed the singular line of the levee and barrier of the port into a sectional and cellular structure which adds multiple lines of redundancy to a new type of system. This system not only provides protection from the forces of the river, but celebrates them in a way which cultivates the rich coexistence of urban and ecological systems. Currently compartmentalized and dispersed land uses are re-integrated so that ports, rails, recreation, refuge, food and fiber production, homes, markets, a school, community facilities, and riparian, swamp, forest, and wetland habitats coexist and overlap in a productive, engaging and sustaining landscape.

Complex systems of redundant small-scale levees allow the river's edge and much port activity to be woven into the urban infrastructure of New Orleans.

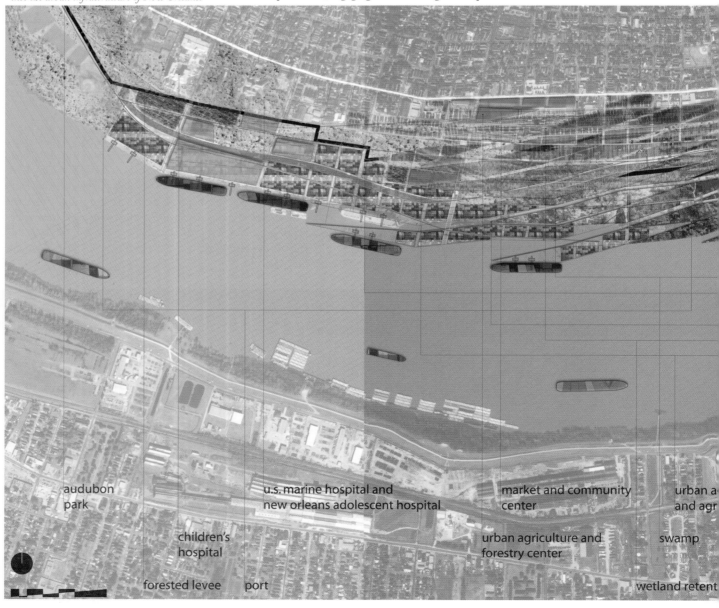

audubon park

children's hospital

forested levee   port

u.s. marine hospital and
new orleans adolescent hospital

market and community
center

urban agriculture and
forestry center

urban a
and agr

swamp

wetland retent

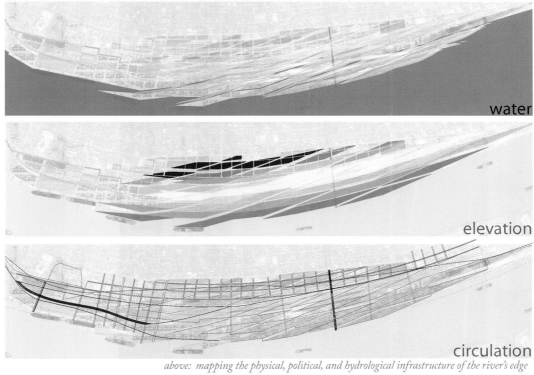

water

elevation

circulation

above: mapping the physical, political, and hydrological infrastructure of the river's edge

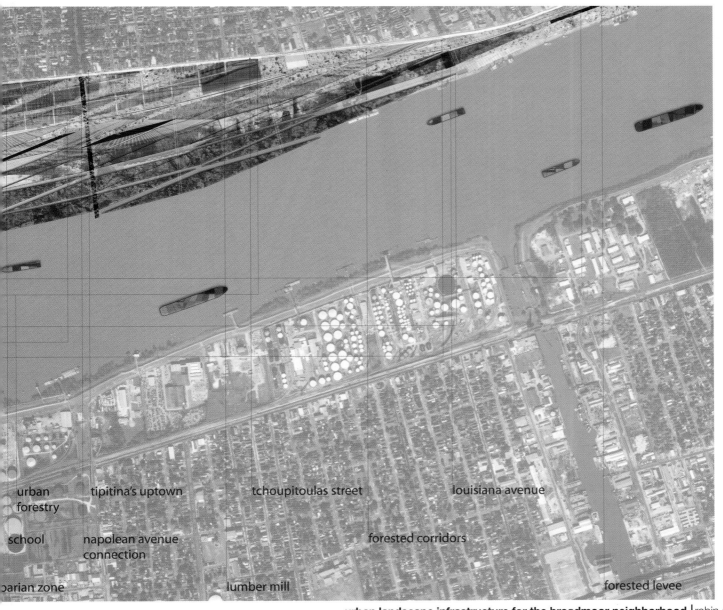

urban
forestry

tipitina's uptown

tchoupitoulas street

louisiana avenue

school

napolean avenue
connection

forested corridors

parian zone

lumber mill

forested levee

urban landscape infrastructure for the broadmoor neighborhood | robin dripps

49

Highway collecting rainwater as beginning of local watershed

Harvested rainwater

New urban park with wetlands retention and filtration systems.

Filtered water distributed to adjacent neighborhoods.

Urban wetlands as public amenity.

Once the largest black Mardi Gras parade route, today the area beneath highways 10 and 90 is populated by parked cars and people sitting on the bases of the columns eating their lunches and playing dominoes. Jazz funerals occasionally pass through and people paint the columns with depictions of lynching, police brutality, and prominent blacks from the neighborhood. Inmates from the nearby jail painted oak trees on the columns as a trace of what had once been a thriving Floral Boulevard.

Before the construction of the elevated highway in 1966, Claiborne Avenue had a 10-block long allee of 250 oak trees, totaling 13 ½ acres. Along this stretch was the largest concentration of black-owned businesses (130) in the country. Pre-Katrina there were 35.

The neighborhoods flanking this site are home to a significant population without personal transportation and there are few opportunities to cross the freeway that slices between them.

During Katrina, these stranded residents sought refuge on the high ground of the highway, pushing shopping carts with their few valuables and suffered in the heat without clean drinking water.

While there is a sense of injustice and tragedy about this landscape, there is also a certain beauty to the complex¬ity of off ramps flying overhead. This scheme heightens this sense of passage on the site - railway, highway, pedestrian promenade, waterflow - creating an exquisite tangle of modali¬ties and scales of movement, making a more complex spatial zone at the interchange.

The site is an underused railyard at the junction of these highways, between Broad Avenue and Claiborne Avenue, adjacent to the Superdome, approximately 130 acres in size. The proposal studies this interchange as wall, ridge, safe zone, high ground, symbol of inequality and watershed, aiming to transform it into a ligament of water and pedestrian infrastructure reconnecting these neighborhoods.

Stormwater runoff from the highway surface is harvested in a forebay to allow the settlement of heavy metals. It is then released through a succession of wetland filtration cells excavated between railways, rinsed through a cypress cell, pumped into overhead distribution lines and finally fed into watertanks. These tanks are placed strategically for access within a network of aerial pedestrian promenades, which may be suspended over a swamp while simultaneously
skimming the underbelly of a freeway. Distribution lines, conflated with walkways, reach beyond the site and touch down in adjacent territories as a primary gesture of reconnection. These tanks are not found only in connection with the aerial walks, but are also present within the two live oak allees that frame the center of the site. A train platform, a shaded bosque for markets, pavilion space, and open fields allow the site to function as a joint between the neighborhoods and give the site a life during non-emergency times.

Residents were returning to Broadmoor as we started the semester. Located at the convergence of New Orleans' radial streets, Broadmoor is a low-lying area. Following Hurricane Katrina, Broadmoor experienced flooding from 2 to 9 feet in depth. In February, we heard that some residents with two-story houses had moved into the upper level (above the flood zone). Some, owning one-story houses, had moved into FEMA trailers parked by their uninhabitable houses. As architects, what could we do to help these residents? While more attention has been focused on other neighborhoods, Broadmoor presents a useful test for anyone thinking of rebuilding New Orleans. Is it possible to live safely and comfortably in a neighborhood that could experience a recurrence of such flooding? Can the problems facing the neighborhood be turned to advantage? A design prepared for such difficult conditions could potentially work in less threatened areas as well. We could create proposals suggesting a new vision for the neighborhood. Following this strategy, we studied the microtopography of flooding in Broadmoor. Two sites that experienced the deepest flood levels became sites for our school proposals.

The choice of a school for this design project was deliberate. Our research had revealed that many residents wanted to return to New Orleans. They were prevented from taking this step because their childrens' schools had not reopened following the hurricane. Yet the city could not afford to reopen the schools because few children had returned. The city was faced with a classic chicken or egg dilemma.

We proposed a Big Picture School to solve this dilemma. Big Picture Schools are small community-based high schools. The Big Picture high schools were started in the mid 1990s by Dennis Littky and Elliot Washor as part of a project to rethink and reform the public schools of Rhode Island. Following the impressive success of the first school in Providence, more schools have been founded based on the same principles. There are now more than 34 Big Picture schools across the country. Students of Big Picture Schools typically spend three days per week in class covering a college preparatory curriculum through self-directed projects. The other two weekdays are spent working with mentors in the community. Such a curriculum, using the talents of young people to work with community leaders, seemed perfectly suited to building back capacity in this de-populated city. The school could grow class by class as students returned.

While the mentor connection is the community's link to the everyday functioning of the school, at the heart of the curriculum is the idea that students learn through solving problems and taking on jobs that matter to the community. So it is significant that the community is invited to quarterly events celebrating student completion of projects. This idea seems especially critical for New Orleans where there is much work needed to understand how to manage a city in such a challenging situation.

Finally, Big Picture Schools are often integrated with their communities through shared facilities. As small schools, less than 300 students, these schools might be less spatially efficient than large schools that are the norm in American public education. One strategy for overcoming the efficiency issue is to share space with institutions or businesses in the community. Sited in New Orleans, the idea of shared resources takes on a new meaning and a new urgency. Asked to make proposals for sharing, students suggested such ideas as a community kitchen, a staging area for construction projects, a park and farmers market, and a community dormitory where homeowners might live while they renovate their property. A school with such resources might serve as a catalyst for rebuilding under difficult circumstances.

A Big Picture High School for Broadmoor

lucia phinney | arch 302 | 3rd year undergraduate architecture studio

4

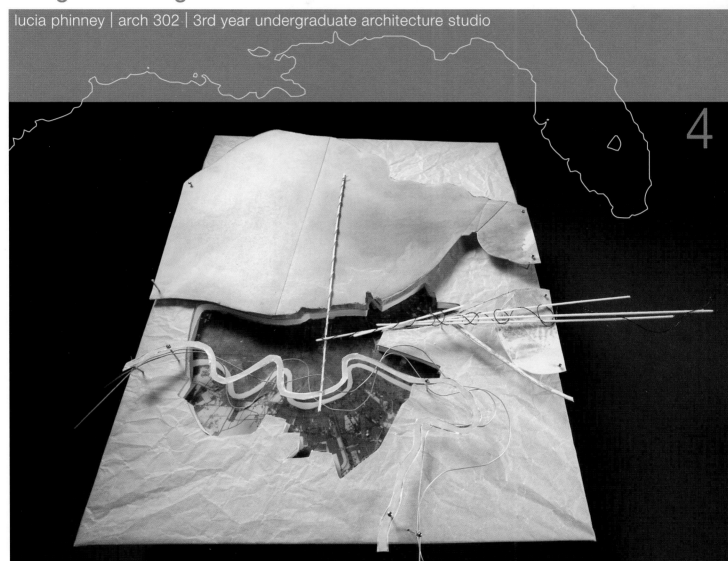

*above : urban analysis of New Orleans: a city at the
edge of Lake Pontchartrain on the Mississippi River*

53

The water catchment system is based on the metaphor of a tree. Water is collected in the canopy and descends through trunks into cisterns below ground. With a supply of fresh water in the cisterns and power from thin film solar cells on the canopies, the school can reopen quickly after a storm.

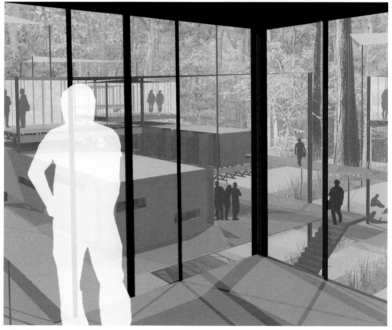

Looking out of the upper level tree house classrooms, students are part of the larger community of the school and the neighborhood. The lightweight materials used to construct the classrooms are easily disassembled for storage when hurricanes approach.

The low lying portion of Broadmoor was a cypress swamp until the early twentieth century. Here, in openings between plank pavers, wetland stripes are replanted with the same swamp species that grew here 100 years ago. These plants mitigate toxins accumulated in post Katrina flooding and eventually form a grand canopy shading a farmers market, gallery, and school. Elevated above river level, these uses can safely occupy the upper layers of this site.

By taking up water from the ground and releasing it through leaves, a tree cools the air by several degrees. Coupled with the shade of the canopy, a tree is a valuable addition to the hot urban climate of New Orleans. This project celebrates the tree by creating a memorial grove of cypress trees. Laced through this grove is a network of elevated structures. Resembling tree houses, or perhaps the camps that formerly lined the shores of Lake Pontchartrain, these structures contain the school program. Elevated terraces provide space for student exhibitions. Shade structures printed with solar cells supply electricity and mitigate the climate until the trees grow to maturity. Rain collectors send potable water to cisterns. The ground level below the school accommodates a farmers market and community celebrations.

Community Dorms
amanda swanekamp

The first building constructed on the site is a dormitory that houses returning families while they renovate their homes. (The structure could later be used as a school-run bed and breakfast.) The school structure is linked to this dormitory by an amphitheater serving school and community alike.

Salvaged cypress protect both buildings from sun and wind. A demountable rain catcher provides shade for the buildings and creates theaters of light and channeled rain that fall through courtyards.

Raised on piers, the school floats above a wetland. Created from the space of abandoned houses, it links to a necklace of flood control wetlands that could thread through Broadmoor.

Large canopies provide much-needed shade while cypress trees grow to maturity. Salvaged cypress screening modulates light and secures the buildings during storms. The elevated buildings provide shade for community space at ground level.

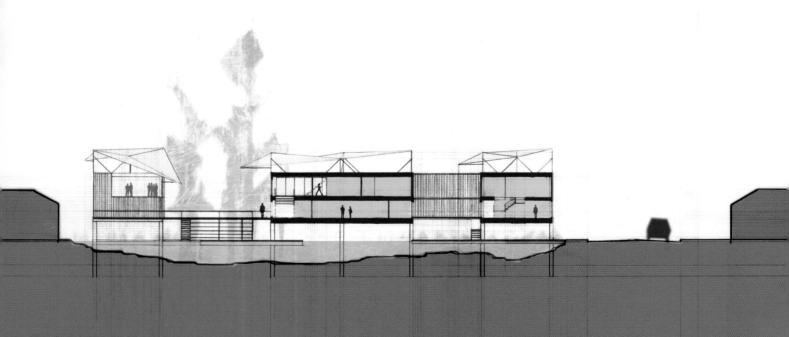

The tent-like classroom structures are built above a constructed wetland that marks the lowest ground in Broadmoor. The placement of the second floor reflects the depth of post-Katrina flooding.

Wetland Laboratory

tamar shafrir

After Hurricane Katrina, could the human inhabitation of the Gulf Coast be considered experimental? Here, classrooms are shelters that connect to different levels of wetland vegetation: the water level, the cattail level, the sub-canopy and canopy levels.

The school is envisioned as a place to investigate the city and its wetland matrix. Rooftop solar collectors provide power, and rain is collected in monumental cisterns anchoring the connection to the neutral ground of Galvez Street. An assembly room facing Galvez serves as the school's gallery and is shared with the community.

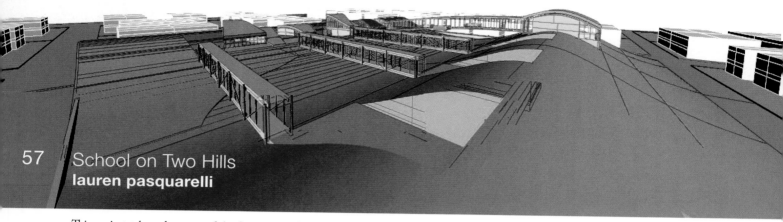

57 | School on Two Hills
lauren pasquarelli

This project takes advantage of the flat terrain of New Orleans to create an exceptional condition: two hills with a view over the city. The hills are shaped by gabion baskets holding salvaged material. This shape is then filled with silt. A wetland lies between the hills and is the focus of a neighborhood park.

Classrooms and work terraces are shaped from one hill. The other houses playing fields and a community center that terminates the neutral ground of Galvez Street. The hills are connected by flexibly programmed bridges. Entrance to the school is made along an outdoor gallery street where students exhibit their work.

Playing fields are embedded in the slope of Milan Hill while a grass-roofed community center rises above to provide safety and refuge. Initially planted with grass, the green slopes will provide dependably dry ground for those tree species that do not survive flooding.

The school program extends through shaded bridges to playing fields on the opposite hill. Floodwater flows away from public spaces into a wetland basin below.

The classrooms have a street presence at the gallery sidewalk along General Pershing Street. Lower spaces are designed for wash-away maintenance after flooding.

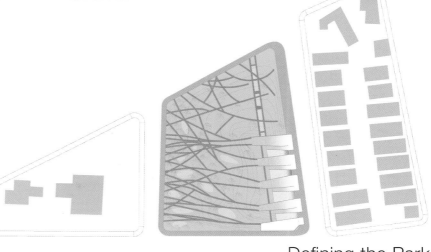

above:
The section reveals a constructed hill that lifts the school above flood level. The classrooms align with rebuilt houses across the street.

The site is planted with cypress trees and defined by paths that weave around wetland pools. The trees that are sparsely planted on the eastern side of the site are dense to the west, their trunks and branches becoming interlaced with climbing nets and play constructions for children.

below:
A dense grove of native bald cypress trees shades the network of paths and pools that define the contours of this urban park.

The school is embedded in a constructed hill facing shotgun houses to the east. Their roofs extend the grass of the park, with a salvaged cypress screen protecting the school from sun and wind. Administration and community spaces line the street front under the classrooms while a corridor stitches through all spaces and links them to Broad Street.

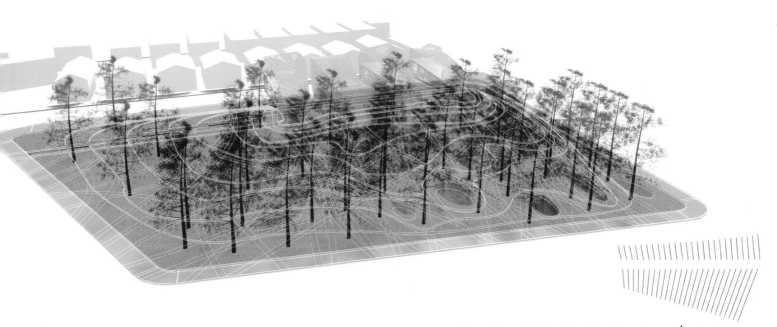

a big picture high school for broadmoor | lucia phinney

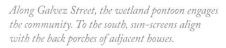

Along Galvez Street, the wetland pontoon engages the community. To the south, sun-screens align with the back porches of adjacent houses.

59 Life Raft
katherine floersheimer

The school structure is inspired by fishing camps along Lake Pontchartrain.

The pontoon structure and canopy provide an island of shade in a flooded city.

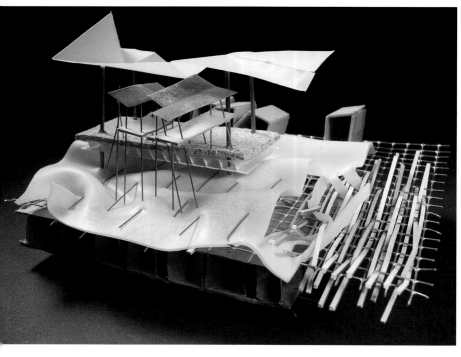

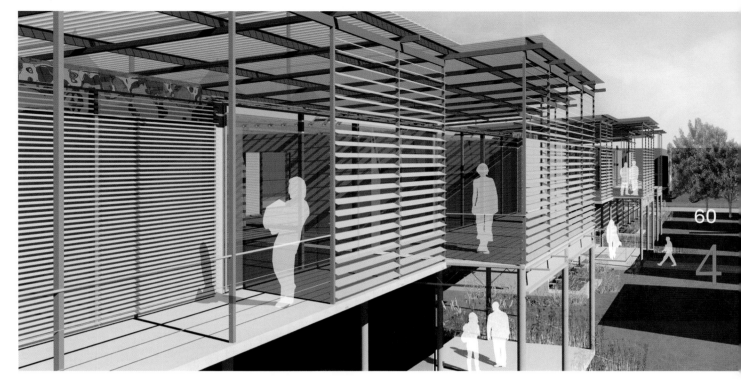

The site is immediately flooded and planted with wetland species to start the remediation process. The edge of this wetland extends the neutral ground of Galvez Street across the site. A pontoon structure spans the wetland at mid-block. Shielded from sun and rain by a demountable canopy, the pontoon can function first as a staging area for reconstruction, then as a community shelter in the wetland park.

The school, shaped to fit the rhythm of existing houses, links to the shelter by rolling stairs. These continue to provide connection as the pontoon moves up and down through seasons of flooding. Permanent school facilities on the upper level shelter open air work terraces and community spaces below. Water collected from the roof is stored in ceiling cisterns that provide thermal mass as well as a reliable source of potable water.

Screens and jalousies modulate the tropical weather.
Cisterns above the classrooms collect water from the roof,
creating and promoting cool conditions and self-sufficiency.

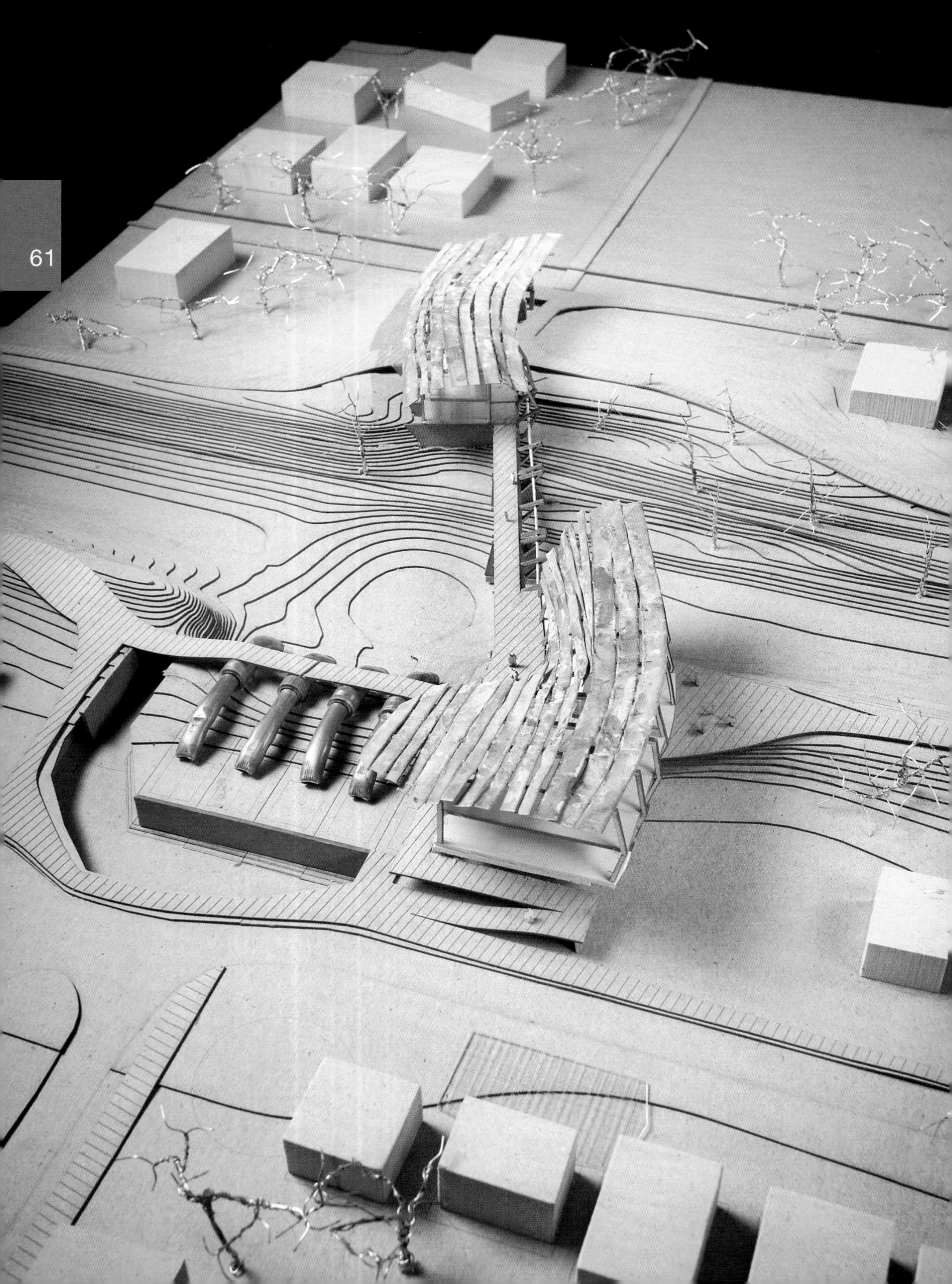

Rebuilding Community on the London Avenue Canal

azadeh rashidi | arch 302 | 3rd year undergraduate architecture studio

5

photo above: London Avenue Canal, by Allison Powell
photo below: infrastructure and scale, by Allison Powell
left: site model, by Owen Howlett

Given the premise that any rebuilding of New Orleans has to begin with the reconstruction of the levees, the goal of this studio was to explore the potential that exists in re-envisioning the drainage infrastructure as a programmable component of the city that is integrated into the urban and social fabric. Through analysis, the students first gained a better understanding of the relationship that exists between the topographic conditions, settlement patterns, infrastructural superimpositions, and socioeconomic divisions that characterize the city. Research on the construction of levees and floodwalls served as a springboard for the design of a community center along the London Avenue Canal.

The center is to establish a new pattern of development in New Orleans that does not merely coexist with the drainage needs of the city, but rather defines the very nature of this system and is inseparable from it. The resulting structure is not necessarily a building, but a more complex landscape that engages the canal, occupying what is now an uninhabited boundary condition in the city, serving to create new connections between the distinct neighborhoods that are divided by the canal, thereby transforming this neutral ground and creating a new intensified relationship to the ebb and flow of water through the city.

Exterior perspective, view of the community center and terraces from the garden.

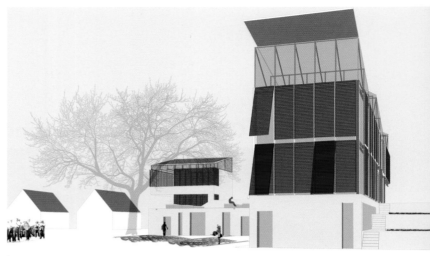

63

Tradition and Improvisation
christina calabrese

A Dillard Neighborhood Community Center

Organized vertically to activate paths that traverse ground and sky, the community center develops procession as the dynamic sequence of spaces that spans site and time. This procession becomes emblematic in light of the present-day situation in New Orleans, where Hurricane Katrina has given a once struggling city the opportunity to being anew.

Brenda Marie Osbey, the Poet Laureate of Louisiana, writes, "The ability not merely to adapt but to improvise is itself inherent in all our notions of tradition. Here [in New Orleans], improvisation is the tradition." The present, or occupied spaces of the community center, communicate between the foundation and sky through adjustable surfaces in the balance between tradition and improvisation.

diagram series: The center is situated in the Dillard neighborhood of New Orleans, which stretches northward from the Gentilly Ridge in a street pattern that is derived from the radiant arpent system, developed by plantation settlements in New Orleans in the nineteenth century. While this system parallels the street fabric of downtown New Orleans, Dillard is an anomaly relative to its immediate context, where development in the early twentieth century was responsible for the regular, orthogonal grid that surrounds the neighborhood.

SETTLEMENT PATTERNS: 1700'S - 1900'S

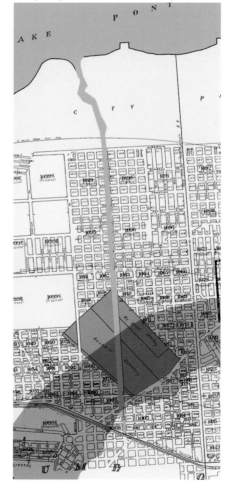

above: exterior perspective, Dillard neighborhood approach.

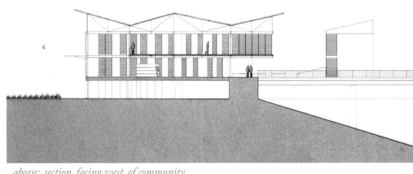

*above: section, facing west, of community
library, classroom spaces, and garden
below: section, facing east, of community clinic,
information center, café, and garden*

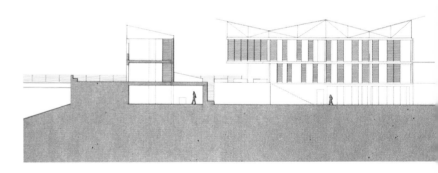

below: exterior perspective, London Avenue Canal approach

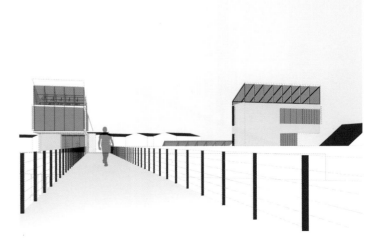

rebuilding community on the london avenue canal |azadeh rashidi

65 Urban Anomalies
greg ericson

Resulting from a contextual study of New Orleans which highlighted anomalies in the urban fabric, this intervention unites the fragmented Dillard neighborhood along the London Avenue Canal and focuses on unique site conditions — a low-lying community garden and towering woodland. The scheme is composed of three main parts: a new canal wall imagined as an animated pedestrian corridor; a folded concrete constructed high ground which addresses the scale of the adjacent neighborhood and garden; and a light steel frame which gestures to the "forest". The project is envisioned as a first move toward re-establishing community along the London Avenue Canal with art studios that open to the canal and a gallery space beneath referencing the artistic history of the neighborhood and making this a destination along the canal. A café becomes a place of refuge and a distribution center for necessities of life in the wake of disaster and the adjacent library serves as a safe-house in times of need.

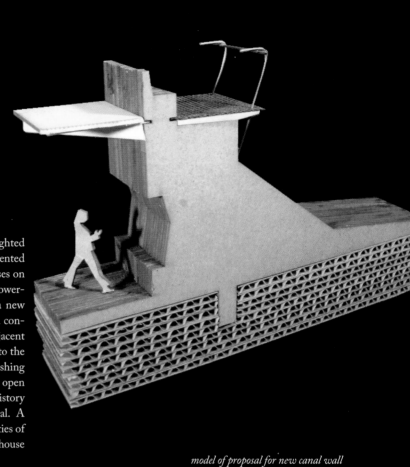

model of proposal for new canal wall

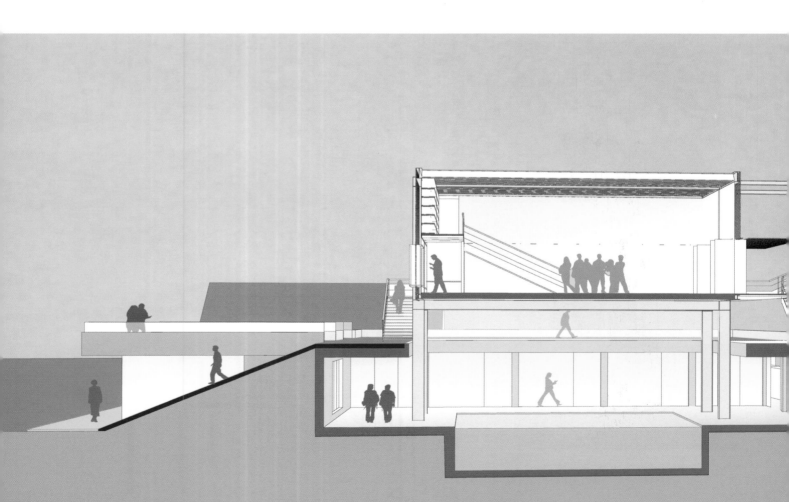

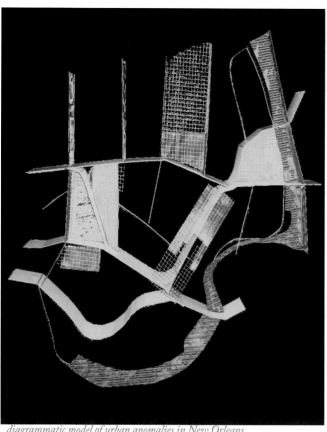

diagrammatic model of urban anomalies in New Orleans.

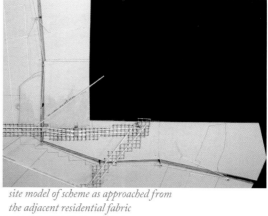

site model of scheme as approached from
the adjacent residential fabric

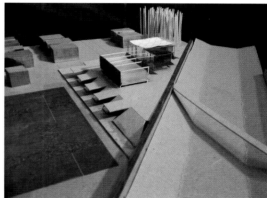

site model of scheme as seen from the canal

longitudinal section from garden level to
canal with forest in the background

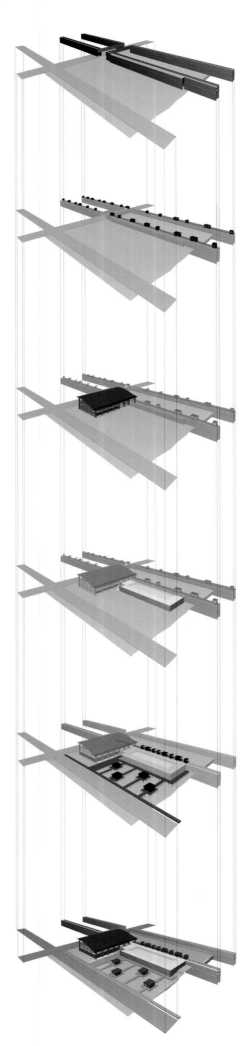

stage 1: *rebuilding of the canal wall*
- thicker, layered canal wall providing better
protection as well as occupiable spaces
(start immediately)

stage 2: *temporary housing units*
- small modular sleeping units to provide temporary
shelter for families coming back to clean and rebuild
(one year to four years)

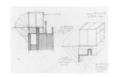

stage 3: *fabrication work zone*
-bottom level houses space for modular housing construc-
tion to rebuild homes destroyed during the storms
- upper level provides elevated refuge
center for protection during storms
(five years)

stage 4: *community pool*
- community recreational space provides opportuni-
ties for community building and growth
- rainwater reuse through biotope system naturally
cleanses water for pool without chemicals
(ten years)

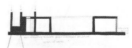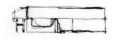

stage 5: *housing units transformed*
- once light-frame units no longer needed for housing,
they are transformed and adapted to be used in other ways
such as shaded units to serve the pool and as classrooms
when four or more are combined to form one space
(ten years)

stage 6: *completed community center*
- complex attracts a wide variety of people for multiple uses
while building community both literally and figuratively

photocollage of London Avenue Canal breach: These photographs were taken six months after Hurricane Katrina and even then little had been done to repair the broken flood wall or clean and rebuild the bordering neighborhood.

sectional model of canal wall and transitional housing unit: This new canal wall design consists of a thickened system of multiple walls and inhabitable spaces. The multiple layers would strengthen the structure and provide a built-in back-up system should one layer fail. In addition to enclosing the canal, the wall would also provide a surface elevated from the toxic layer of sediment to install transitional housing units for residents wanting to rebuild.

With the proposal for a new neighborhood community center in the recently-devastated city of New Orleans, an intriguing question arose, how does one make a community center for a community that no longer exists? In an effort to keep in mind the fact that many families relocated after the storm, leaving most neighborhoods in need of complete rebuilding of both their homes and communities, the intention of this project is to design a plan of redevelopment with the idea of rebuilding homes to rebuild community. The proposed plan would be carried out during the next 5-10 years beginning with the most immediate and pressing needs of safety and shelter and then continuing onto the more general area of community-building.

In order for residents to feel safe enough to return, the first step in the rebuilding process would be to reconstruct the flood wall with a more structurally sound design. Prefabricated transitional housing units would then be installed to be used by returning families while they rebuild. The next stage of the project would include the construction of a community building which would serve the residents as a construction center to assist in the rebuilding efforts and also provide a safe place of refuge during future storms. Once the community has rebuilt their homes, the temporary housing and construction center would be transformed into a community center featuring a swimming pool, classroom spaces, and a library to serve the local residents.

Community on the Canal
Levee as Public Space
jp mays

This design is inspired by the idea of a folded plane that pulls from the urban residential context and leads to the canal, viewing it as a destination rather than a barrier. By remaking the levee as a double-berm redundant flood system that also functions as parkland and creating a center that spans this space, the canal is no longer ignored.

The center establishes a connection between neighborhood and canal, and operates as a community refuge, both daily and in times of emergency. There are numerous levels to support the multiplicity of the program, including an outdoor theater, classrooms, a library, and childcare, all under an arching shade canopy that shields occupants from both harsh summer sun and frequent showers.

right: transportation diagram of bus routes and parking, overlaid on high- and low-income areas

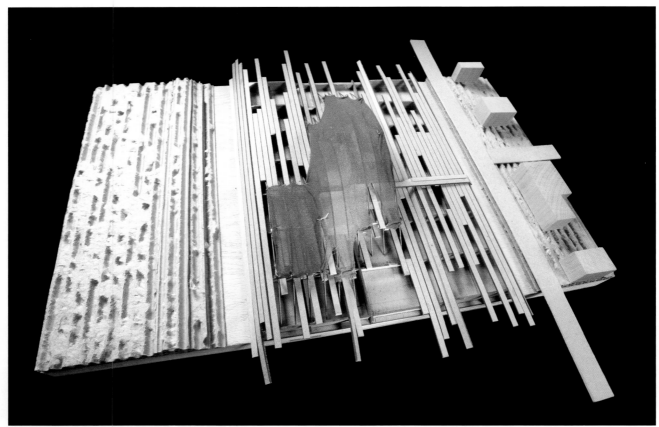

This study model was an important step in reaching the final design, establishing the canopy and further developing the concept of connecting to the constructed landscape.

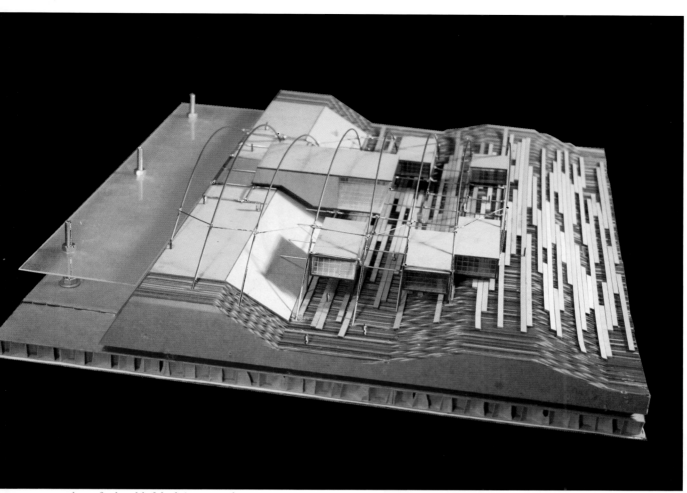

above: final model of the design proposal

*below: series of study models: initial study models illustrate
the double-berm levee and the connection to the canal*

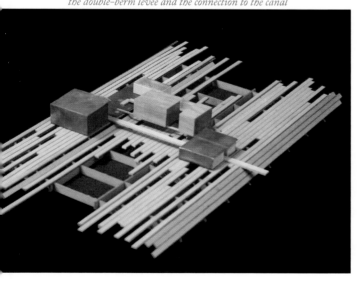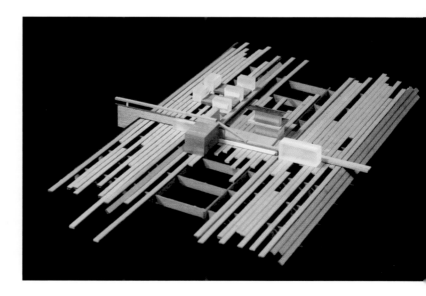

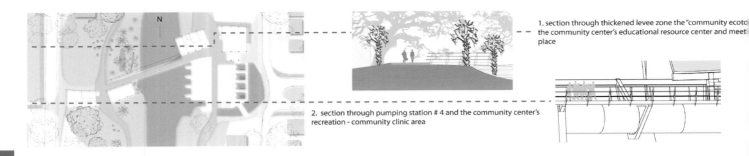

1. section through thickened levee zone the "community ecoto the community center's educational resource center and meet place

2. section through pumping station # 4 and the community center's recreation - community clinic area

Connections | Filmore & St. Anthony
owen howlett

The proposed community center, located on the site of pumping station #4 is both an elevated place and a connector between places -- neighborhoods which are currently isolated by London Avenue Canal's levee walls. This site strategy, and the network of canal-side pedestrian greenways it makes possible, is part of a larger vision for aligning the interests of community and New Orleans' infrastructure.

This method of creating occupiable boundary zones, fully expressive of the dialectic between human occupation and environment, will adapt the city to the changing relationships of land-sea, resource conservation and use, and, on an elemental level, between man and the natural environment.

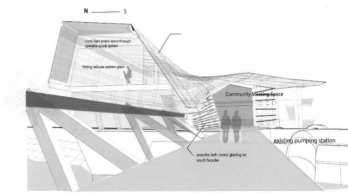

above: climate and materials: South facing roof plane collects energy. Existing grid is connected and conduit is lofted across canal along circulation route. Site commensalisms: there is reciprocity of resource dynamics.

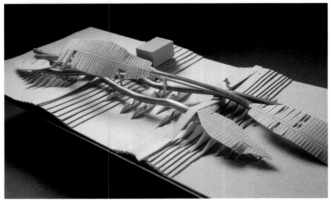

above: abstract study model: Initial design efforts were directed toward making very strong, 'rooted' connections with the unstable ground condition and providing generous, self-sustaining canopies for shelter, community-making and energy collection; two fundamental conditions New Orleans needs. These conditions were considered in relationship with the existing and potential infrastructural and circulation flows on site, (represented in copper conduit) creating a synergetic and dynamic place.

below: longitudinal section is cut through pumping station and clinic and exercise facility (pedestrian connector and arts complex in elevation) In contrast with the typical levee cross sections of New Orleans, ones that failed in the floods of Hurricane Katrina, the site section across the London Avenue Canal thickens levee walls with both a building program and a planted barrier zone of cypress and palmetto. The levee becomes more structurally secure and is enriched by a layer of programmatic and ecologic functionality.

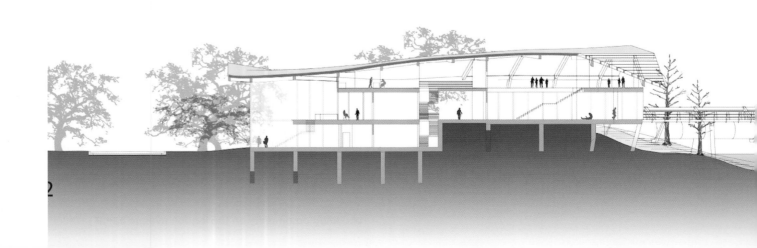

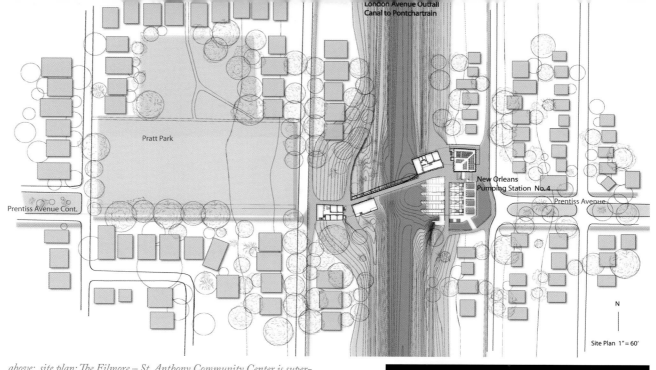

Site Plan 1" = 60'

above: site plan: The Filmore – St. Anthony Community Center is super-
imposed over an existing pumping station (New Orleans #4) that draws
water from underground canals under East and West Prentiss Avenues.
Despite this massive infrastructural connection across London Avenue
Canal, the neighborhoods on each side are isolated and demographically
distinct (as evident in the different size of houses on each side). The proposed
community center includes performance and art spaces, an educational
resource center, and health clinic and recreational facilities: making a
place of social and infrastructural convergence out of a former divide.

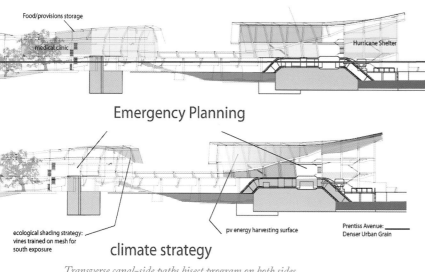

Food/provisions storage

medical clinic

Hurricane Shelter

Emergency Planning

ecological shading strategy:
vines trained on mesh for
south exposure

pv energy harvesting surface

Prentiss Avenue:
Denser Urban Grain

climate strategy

Transverse canal-side paths bisect program on both sides
of the canal, covered mezzanine spaces are located about
these intersections, enriching the manifest "boundary
conditions" and serving as ventilating "dogtrots"

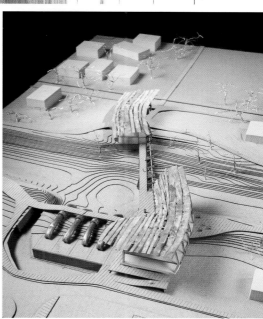

above: site model: The subtle changes in topography on site,
critical to the integration of the community center within
its infrastructural context, were best represented through
a physical topography model with layers for every foot
of grade change on site. The photograph shows an aerial
view west of the canal pumping station across to Pratt
Park. Patinated metal roof surfaces represent a solar energy
collecting surface-a critical element of the sites self-sufficiency.

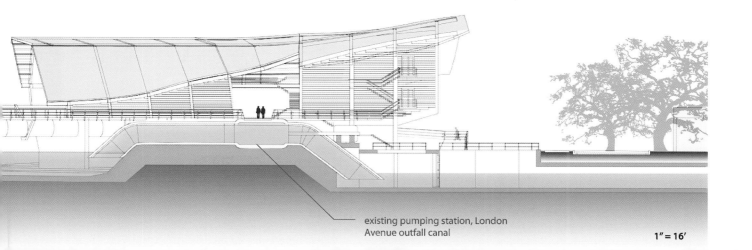

existing pumping station, London
Avenue outfall canal

1" = 16'

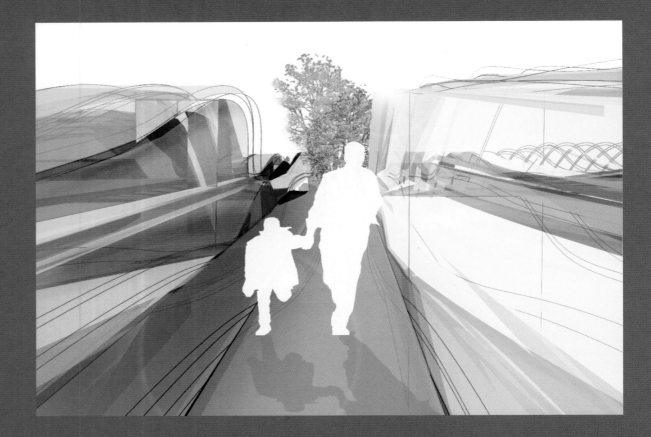

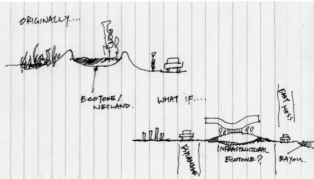

reverted ecotone > safe haven

ecotone> landscape striation

An ecotone is a transition area between two adjacent ecological communities (ecosystems). It may appear on the ground as a gradual blending of the two communities across a broad area, or it may manifest itself as a sharp boundary line.

Opportunity.

This project presupposes that new urban land use strategies in New Orleans will favor the location of public buildings, in particular schools, on high ground. In a given Faubourg, these sites would also become the centers for community organization in emergencies. These sites would serve as areas of refuge as well as pedagogical models for good water management practices at small and medium scales.

Another opportunity was seen as the celebration of water through the entire section of these sites in the architecture as well as the landscape as they work in conjunction as a system.

Finally, the effects of high winds and the powerful sun and humidity in New Orleans were studied as other layers in the development of the designs.

SITE

The particular site was chosen because it was a dry oasis surrounded by water after Katrina while also being very close to some of the most devastated areas of the city. Located in Faubourg Bayou St. John, the site is nestled in the crook made by Bayou St. John as it veers east then south again on the southeast corner of City Park. This site also required a critical look at the canals as weak points in the city's infrastructure while at the same time presenting some of the most potentially impacting solutions for the environmental and urban issues that face New Orleans.

PROGRAM

The program for the project was an early childhood education center (a daycare center and preschool) and an area of refuge. Students were encouraged to develop adjunct programs such as neighborhood parks. Another possible component of the project asked if these sites could serve as temporary housing for residents of the neighborhoods as they worked towards rehabilitating or rebuilding their homes and neighborhoods.

TECTONICS

Imagining a building's section as described by a canopy (its sky condition) at its highest elevations and a mat (its ground condition) in the lowest elevations, the projects were charged with integrating issues of absorption as well as shading and stability.

The added programmatic requirement of an area of refuge brought with it the questions of how to design for both extreme wind and flooding. Students were asked to think of strategies for occupying higher planes and for spaces that were described by thickened protective layers.

THE INVESTIGATIONS

Some students studied plants that adapt well to watery conditions such as Anna Lucey and Sarah Ramsey. Others, such as Hank Byron, concentrated on incorporating many speeds and methods of absorption of water in order to create a system that can hold water within it, manage water, and use much larger volumes of the water that lands on the site. Finally, others such as Alex Kong studied larger-scale urban strategies by proposing multi-tasking infrastructural systems that serve their infrastructural purposes while also providing the stabilizing membranes necessary to build, completing ecological loops and separating the individual Faubourg from its dependence on larger regional input.

left: drawings by Alex Kong

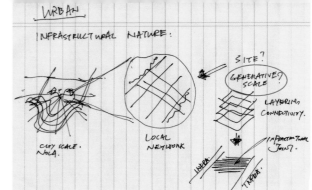

:matnopy
-a single underlying infrastructure

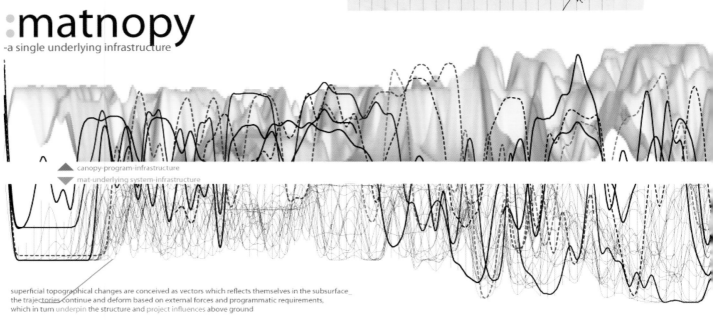

▲ canopy-program-infrastructure
▼ mat-underlying system-infrastructure

superficial topographical changes are conceived as vectors which reflects themselves in the subsurface_
the trajectories continue and deform based on external forces and programmatic requirements,
which in turn underpin the structure and project influences above ground

environmental factors > solar > programming > density
form: heat, energy, light, uv radiation

programmatic space within the site is laid out according to time
table, of which different programmatic spaces require different
amount of sunlight for different durations.
from all the information gathered, programmatic
density is then determined according to the overall
solar demand and locations.

dune fomation according to solar demand >

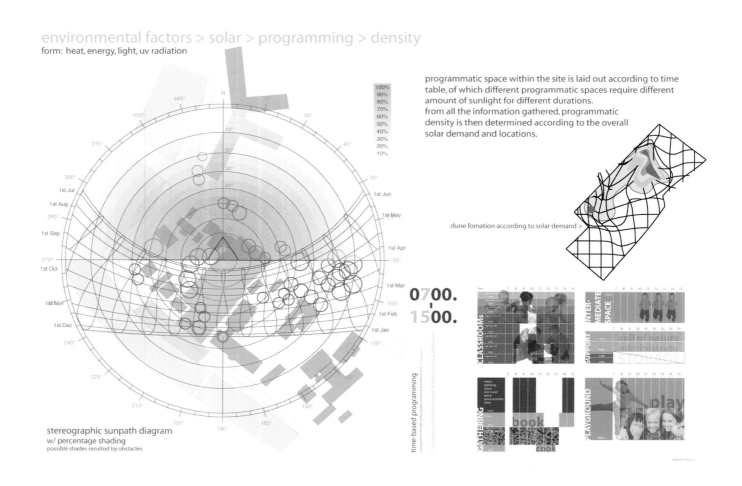

stereographic sunpath diagram
w/ percentage shading
possible shades resulted by obstacles

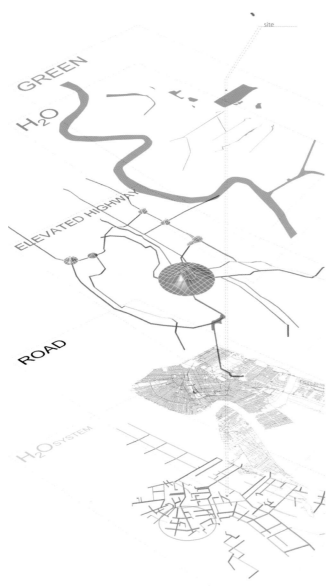

GREEN

H₂O

ELEVATED HIGHWAY

ROAD

H₂O SYSTEM

site

alex kong

An experiment on landscape/infrastructural urbanism in post-Katrina New Orleans

"In conceptualizing a more organic, fluid urbanism, ecology itself becomes an extremely useful lens through which to analyze and project alternative urban futures."
Terra Fluxus, James Corner

"Landscape is not only a formal model for urbanism today, but perhaps more importantly, a model for process."
Mat Urbanism: the thick 2D, Stan Allen

Matnopy – a hybrid mix between mat urbanism and canopies, there is no interruption from open landscape to built urbanism, namely architecture. This suggests shifting attention away from the object qualities of space to the systems that condition the distribution and density of infrastructure and urban form. Located by the Bayou St. John in New Orleans because it is high ground, the site did not suffer from the flooding that accompanied Katrina. Because of its unique location both geographically and infrastructurally, a systemic deployment is chosen to facilitate the site becoming a safe haven rather than the development of a formal building mass on site. Taken into account the existing land condition and by speculating possible overflow of the bayou, a striated landscape is conceived to contain refuges for vegetation, animals and also people. Where the undulation is tall enough to accommodate human beings, it also serves as an outdoor classroom (cocoon-like habitation) for the pre-school that will occupy part of the later "emerging space". Rather than avoiding its peripheral environmental resources and infrastructure, ponds and water retention systems are located within the landscape along with two aqueducts.

These infrastructural pipes not only carry water connecting the city's utility grid and the natural hydrology of the bayou, they are also comprised of synthetic structural materials that ultimately emerge above ground and become foundations for later construction. The so-called "mat foundation" is made up of bundles of carbon fibers cable (springing from the aqueduct), pre-stressed reinforcing bars and reinforced concrete which create a stable yet flexible groundwork for the programs above ground. Landscape becomes a medium to mediate architecture and infrastructure. Indeed, the idea of biotic landscape as a model for urbanism is considered. "Nature" is redefined in a non-linear fashion and a brand new morphological pattern of urban settlement is suggested for post-Katrina New Orleans. While both ecological and urban processes are happening simultaneously on the site, complex networks emerge from the city's infrastructures and constantly reiterate the inseparable relationship between landscape and urbanism.

environmental factors > wind > programming > d
prevailing wind > natural ventilation

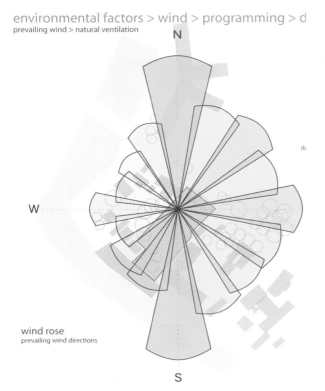

N

W

S

dt

wind rose
prevailing wind directions

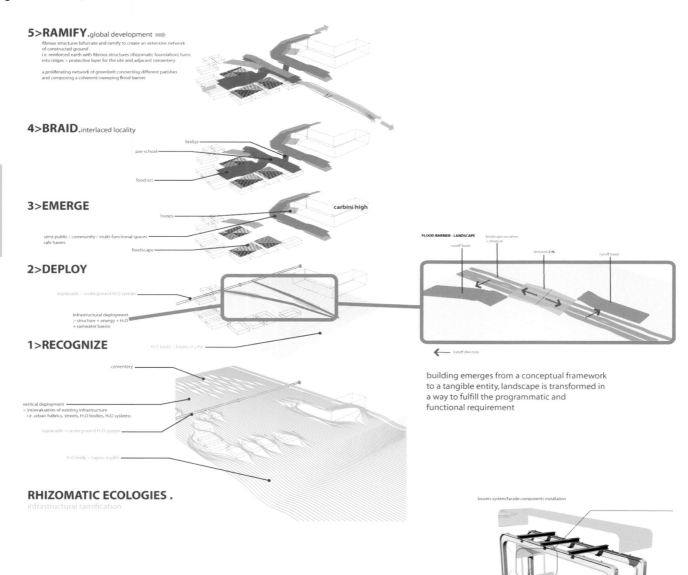

5>RAMIFY.global development ➡

fibrous structures bifurcate and ramify to create an extensive network of constructed ground
i.e. reinforced earth with fibrous structures (rhizomatic foundation) turns into ridges > protective layer for the site and adjacent cementery

a proliferating network of greenbelt connecting different parishes and composing a coherent/sweeping flood barrier

4>BRAID.interlaced locality

bridge
pre-school
food/sci.

3>EMERGE

carbini high

hoops

semi-public / community / multi-functional spaces
safe haven

foodscape

FLOOD BARRIER - LANDSCAPE
landscape transition > structure
runoff basin
elevated 2 FL.
runoff basin

2>DEPLOY

esplanade > underground H₂O system

infrastructural deployment
> structure + energy + H₂O
+ rainwater basins

runoff direction

1>RECOGNIZE

H₂O body - bayou st john

building emerges from a conceptual framework to a tangible entity, landscape is transformed in a way to fulfill the programmatic and functional requirement

cementery

vertical deployment
> (re)evaluation of existing infrastructure
i.e. urban frabrics, streets, H₂O bodies, H₂O systems

esplanade > underground H₂O system

H₂O body - bayou st john

RHIZOMATIC ECOLOGIES .
infrastructural ramification

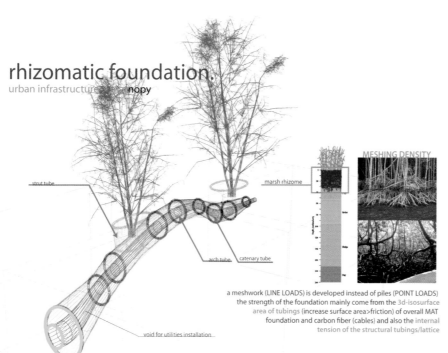

rhizomatic foundation.
urban infrastructure nopy

strut tube

marsh rhizome

arch tube.   catenary tube

void for utilities installation

MESHING DENSITY

a meshwork (LINE LOADS) is developed instead of piles (POINT LOADS)
the strength of the foundation mainly come from the 3d-isosurface area of tubings (increase surface area>friction) of overall MAT foundation and carbon fiber (cables) and also the internal tension of the structural tubings/lattice

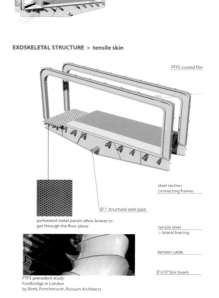

louvers system/facade components installation

cross ventilation is introduced by the permeable surface over metal floor
the cantilevered portion of the building will also be coated doc whereas a dehumidifier must be installed to avoid too high rela

EXOSKELETAL STRUCTURE > tensile skin

PTFE-coated fibe

steel section connecting frames

Ø 1' structural steel pipe

perforated metal panels allow breeze to get through the floor plane

tensile steel
> lateral bracing

tension cable

8"x10" box beam

PTFE precedent study:
Footbridge in London
by Birds, Portchmouth, Russum Architects

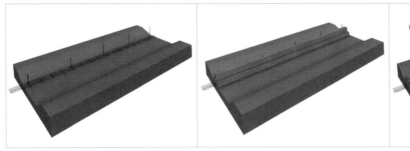

rebars and formworks are laid out to cast
the concrete footing

>>>>>

rebars are placed inside the concrete formwork to create
a curved reinforced concrete slab;

compression strength of stone + tensile strength of steel
concrete slab touches the ground and between the intermediate material
which holds together the re-bars from underground to aboveground.
it acts like an elongated piece of concrete footing, of which the curved-up
portion allows connection with the cantilevered part of the building

Mat.nopy_NOLA 78

alex kong

6

"Nature" is redefined in a non-linear fashion and a brand new morphological pattern
of urban settlement is suggested for post-Katrina New Orleans. While both ecological and urban processes are happening simultaneously on the site, complex networks
emerge from the city's infrastructures and constantly reiterate the inseparable relationship between landscape and urbanism.

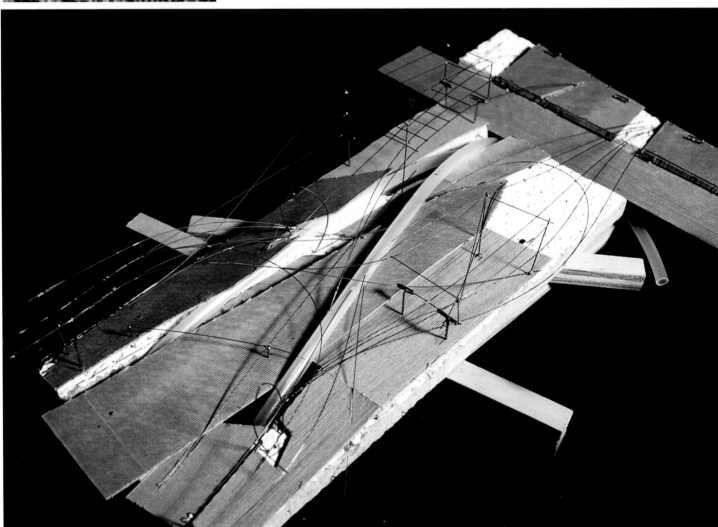

experimental model studying surfacing and in-
frastructural connectionsabove:

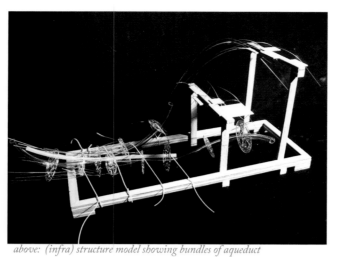

above: (infra) structure model showing bundles of aqueduct

section a-a'

section b-b'

rhizomatic foundation.>rhizomatic spaceframe_structural transition
urban infrastructure > building infrastructure > matnopy
SYSTEM BECOMING OTHER SYSTEMS......

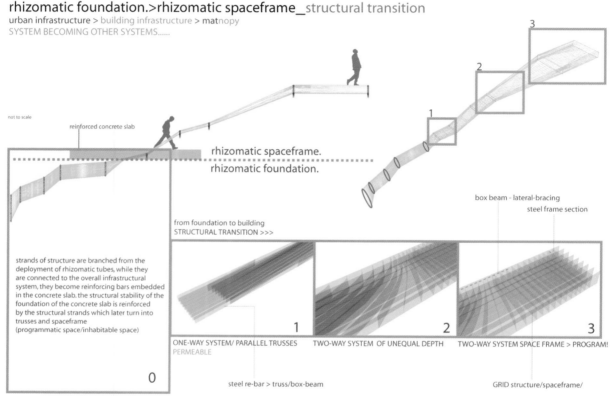

not to scale

reinforced concrete slab

rhizomatic spaceframe.
rhizomatic foundation.

from foundation to building
STRUCTURAL TRANSITION >>>

strands of structure are branched from the deployment of rhizomatic tubes, while they are connected to the overall infrastructural system, they become reinforcing bars embedded in the concrete slab. the structural stability of the foundation of the concrete slab is reinforced by the structural strands which later turn into trusses and spaceframe
(programmatic space/inhabitable space)

0

box beam - lateral-bracing

steel frame section

1
ONE-WAY SYSTEM/ PARALLEL TRUSSES
PERMEABLE

2
TWO-WAY SYSTEM OF UNEQUAL DEPTH

3
TWO-WAY SYSTEM SPACE FRAME > PROGRAM!

steel re-bar > truss/box-beam

GRID structure/spaceframe/

rhizomatic infrastructure > H₂O redistribution > drainage

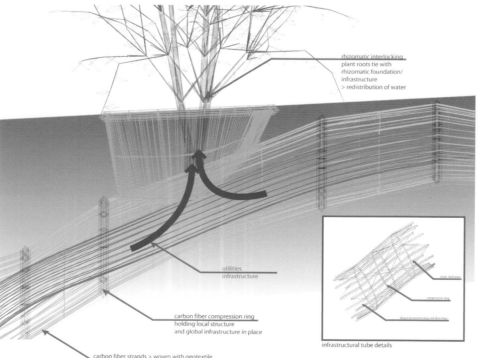

rhizomatic interlocking
plant roots tie with
rhizomatic foundation/
infrastructure
> redistribution of water

utilities
infrastructure

carbon fiber compression ring
holding local structure
and global infrastructure in place

carbon fiber strands > woven with geotextile

infrastructural tube details

H₂O redistribution

IN

OUT

The utility pipe running inside the infrastructural tube can redistribute water according to difference in water content. Subsiding ground condition can be reduced by directing water to vegetations.

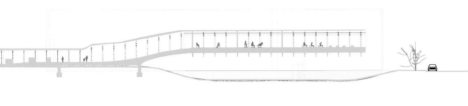

above: perspective views show community center, adjunct programs, and theater
below: perspective view show "energyscape" - spanning over Bayou St. John

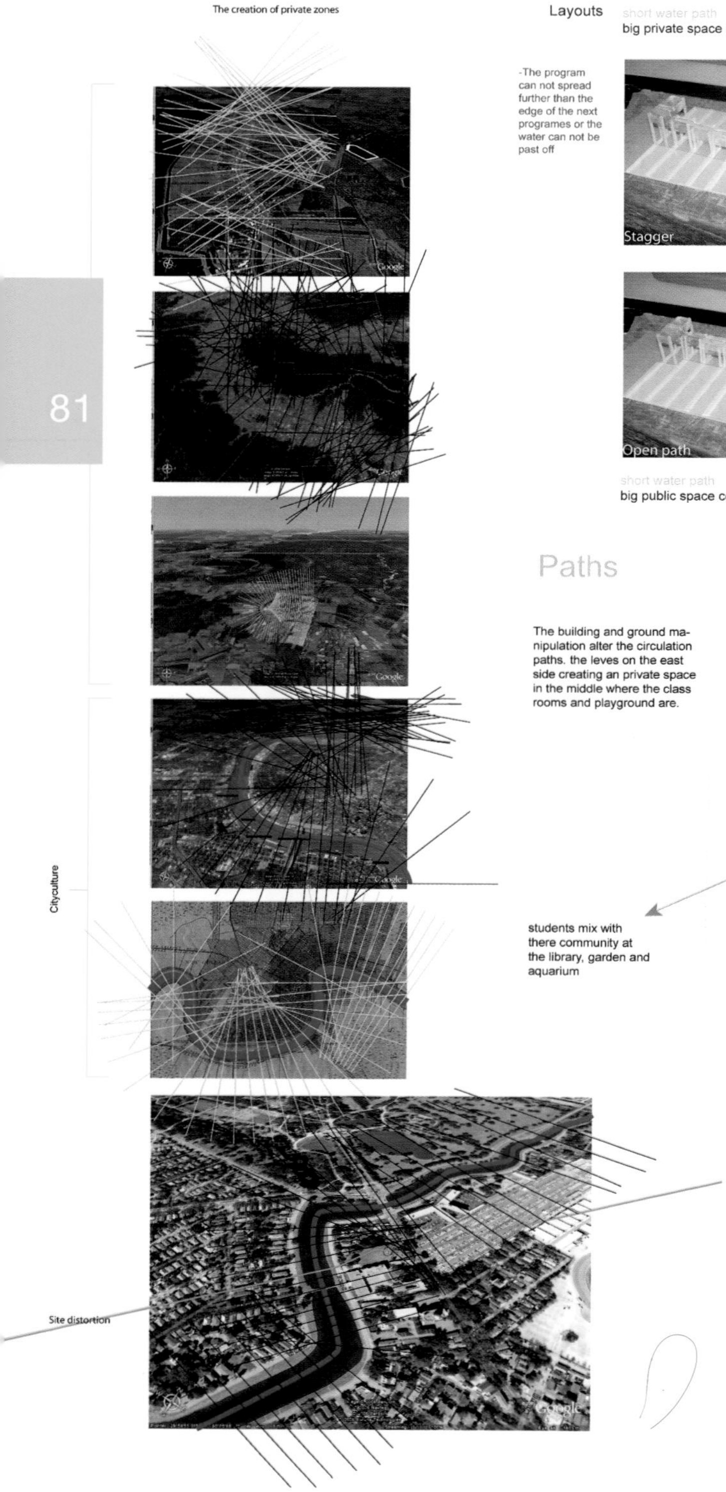

81

The creation of private zones

Cityculture

Site distortion

Layouts

-The program can not spread further than the edge of the next programes or the water can not be past off

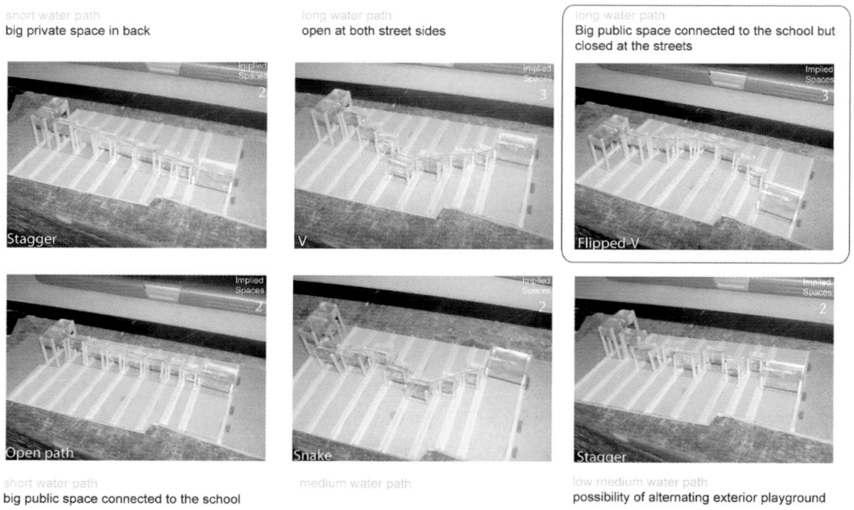

short water path
big private space in back

long water path
open at both street sides

long water path
Big public space connected to the school but closed at the streets

Implied Spaces

Stagger

V

Flipped-V

Implied Spaces

Open path

Snake

Stagger

short water path
big public space connected to the school

medium water path

low medium water path
possibility of alternating exterior playground

Paths

The building and ground manipulation alter the circulation paths. the leves on the east side creating an private space in the middle where the class rooms and playground are.

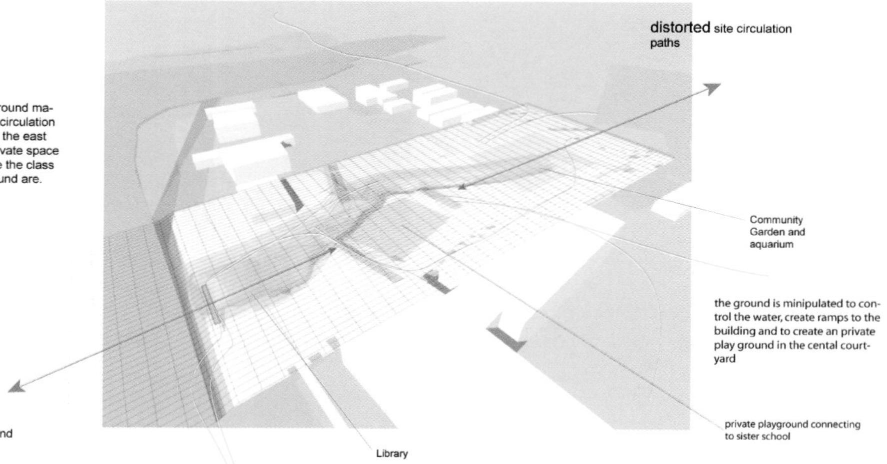

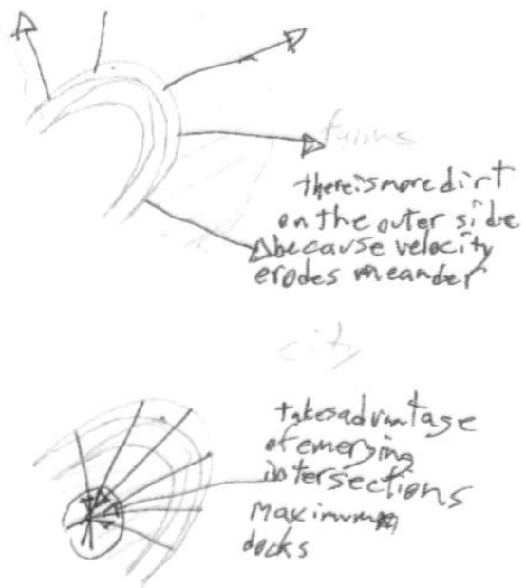

distorted site circulation paths

Community Garden and aquarium

the ground is minipulated to control the water, create ramps to the building and to create an private play ground in the cental courtyard

students mix with there community at the library, garden and aquarium

private playground connecting to sister school

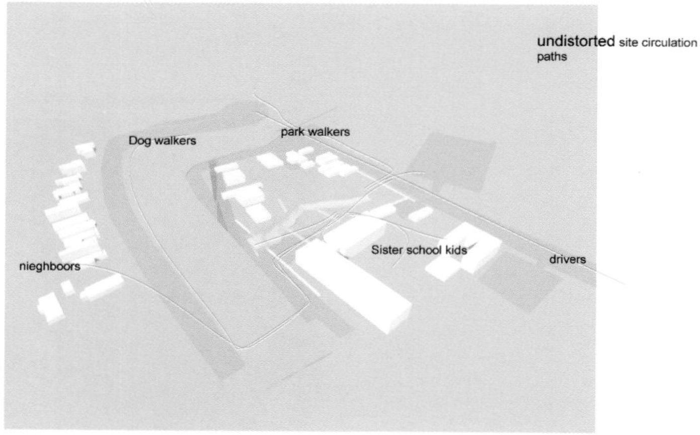

Library

undistorted site circulation paths

Dog walkers

park walkers

nieghboors

Sister school kids

drivers

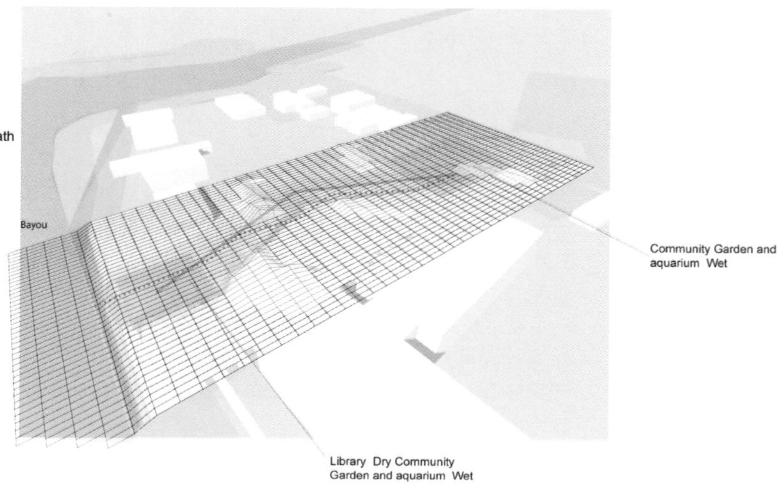

there is more dirt on the outer side because velocity erodes meander

takeadvantage of emerging intersections Maximum decks

...... ground path
——— roof path

Bayou

Community Garden and aquarium Wet

Library Dry Community Garden and aquarium Wet

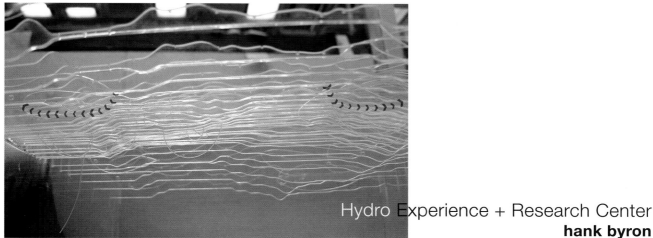

study model: underground water paths

The Mississippi river meanders in order to find the shortest path to the ocean. This is also reinforced by how the levees concentrate the water into a linear path for efficient use of materials and to allow for the quickest shipping routes. This logic does not allow for the land to absorb some of the water and can lead to sinking land.

The proposed site for an elementary school is on high ground so the intervention is focused on its own rainwater. The proposal still does not repel all of the water, instead the site is divided into areas that can store water and places that are protected from water. This is done through the manipulation of the contours and also the lifting of program to different elevations. "Land bumps" or bioswales are staggered to slow the water. They also serve as circulation ramps to the enclosed portions of the program. The bump closest to the water is turned into an amphitheater. The building however is bent into a "V" to extend the path of the water on the roof and to shade the outdoor courtyard. The roof is covered with grass to further absorb water and also connects to programmatic outlets that use the rainwater. The rainwater however can be polluted so another system is used for the programs that need cleaner water. The cleaner water is collected from the air and a dehumidification system works by using water that is cooled using a geothermal system. This water comes up and into the coldest and least humid parts of the program such as the library and classrooms.

Water Context

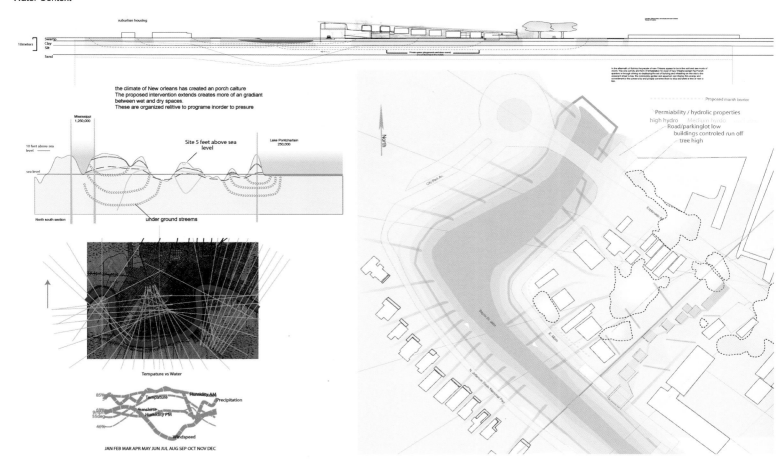

a high school for higher ground | cecilia hernandez nichols

Sectional drawing through the site

right: conceptual model
below: Exploded Axon – construction sequence

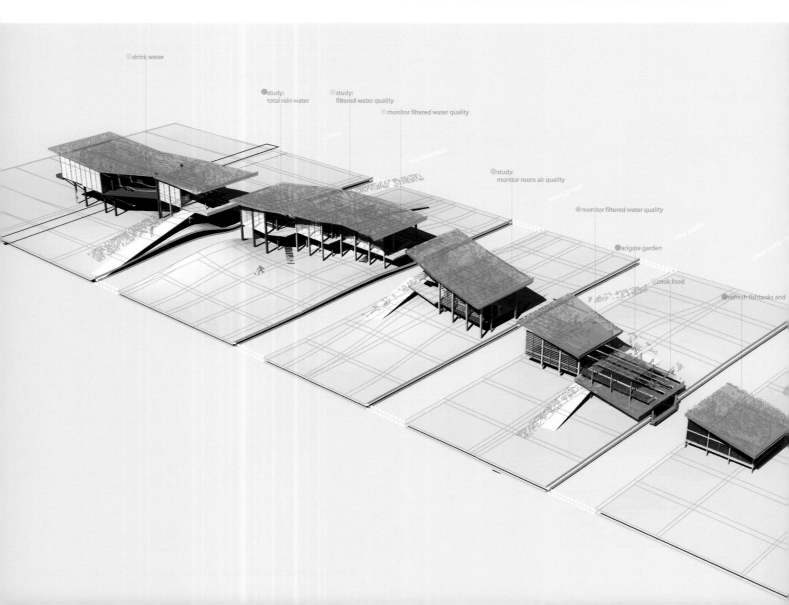

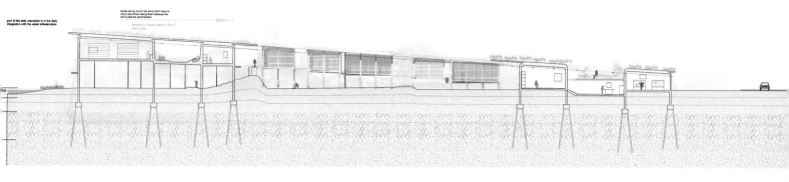

In the aftermath of Katrina, the people of New Orleans appear to be in the wait and see mode of shock. The only activity and form of inhabitation for most of New Orleans except the French quarter is through driving so displaying the act of building and inhabiting on this site to the Esplanade Street is key, the community garden and aquarium can display this energy and commitment to the passers by and possibly convince them to stop and plant a tree or raise a fish.

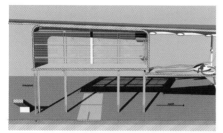

SIPS panels are used on the interior of the roof allowing for insulation and greater structural integrity.

The green roof is a place for kids to grow plants, water to be filtered, and works to cool the building.

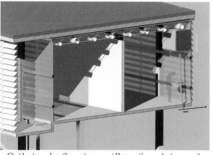

Coil pipe, hecflex pipe, oscillates from being a closed system in the interior spaces from coming directly in contact with the body on the exterior spaces to create furniture.

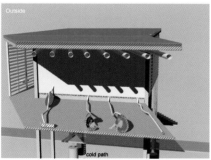

PVC pipe follows the under-side of the roof. On the exterior it becomes completely closed so it does not allow air from the interior to flow outside.

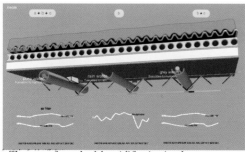

The water from the dehumidification is collected on the bottom pvc pipe.

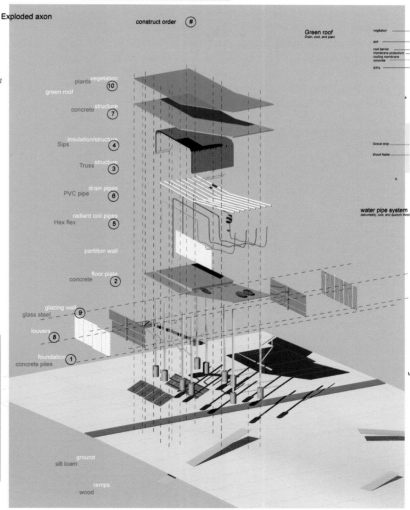

Exploded axon

construct order (#)

Green roof
Drain, cool, and plant

vegetation
soil
root barrier
membrane protection
roofing membrane
concrete
SIPs

plants — vegetation (10)
green roof

concrete — structure (7)

insulation/structure
Sips (4)

Truss — structure (3)

PVC pipe — drain pipes (6)

Hex flex — radiant coil pipes (5)

partition wall

concrete — floor plate (2)

glass steel — glazing wall (9)

louvers (8)

concrete piles — foundation (1)

Gravel stop
Wood Nailer

water pipe system
dehumidity, cool, and quench thirst

ground
silt loam

ramps
wood

Photoselective screens are used in farming to turn UV light into visible light, triggering morphologies in plants. They are used in project | mangrove to provide shade and protection from rain while retaining a close relationship with the outdoors. The pile foundations paired with a semi-permeable canopy are a nod to the indigenous mangrove tree.

Project _ Mangrove
anna lucey

Project_mangrove is a preschool in the city of New Orleans, located at the knuckle of Bayou Saint John. The site is a unique crossroads of historically significant buildings, pre-existing schools, and topographic features (namely the ridge that runs through the north of the site). Using the indigenous mangrove tree as inspiration, the design addresses the delicate balance of earth, water, and sky. The decision to use the mangrove tree springs from a desire to incorporate the native natural design into built structure. This strategy takes cues from the successful flora and fauna in the region to deal with a sensitive site. The site was redefined as starting at the bayou that is now allowed to penetrate the school and peninsula. Esplanade is diverted around the site.

The building complex consists of an east wing and a west wing, with a classroom block running the length of the east wing. When meeting the ground, the classrooms employ a foundation strategy that reflects the root system of the mangrove tree; one that lends it strength and stability in an area where the ground condition is not always reliable. The foundation begins with deep piles (trunk) in a concrete-infill method. The top slabs in the classrooms are a large-sediment terrazzo pour, reminding occupants of the elements beneath them, much like the mangrove shows its roots.

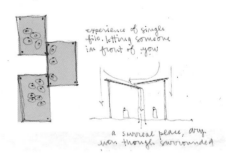

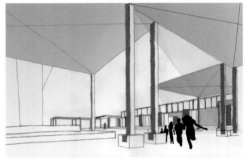

below: The student drop off point is a stepped landscape that engages students, teachers, and caretakers at all scales through the incorporation of raised cement blocks that range from one foot to two feet in height.

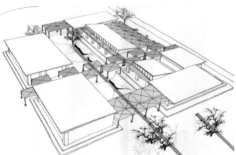

above: The photoselective roofs and screens make for a dynamic landscape where the juxtapositions between light and shadow, cool and warm, and dry and wet move the individual from one place to another.

interior perspective: the sun screen system retains
views outdoors while blocking the harsh sun and grade
beams playfully sweep through the interior spaces.

Pathways Preschool
sarah ramsey

As a Montessori school, Pathways Preschool centers itself around providing its young students with a sense of independence anchored in a strong school community. The school is designed to function as a neighborhood school, envisioning students arriving on foot from nearby homes. The concept of threshold is a key one. A porous design fosters a sense of community and encourages a connection with the outdoors. Each classroom has individual access to the school's outdoor space. Deep overhangs provide protected outdoor areas while a sun screen system helps shade classrooms from a hot southern sun.

The school is also an exploration into Post-Katrina building strategies. Recognizing the instability of the ground in New Orleans, Pathways Preschool employs a twofold interlocking foundation system. A network of post-tensioned grade beams stabilizes the silty ground, while a series of anchor piles locks the building into place. These grade beams remain visible on the ground plane, tracing a didactic story of structure, and extend beyond the building boundary, providing a system for shaping the surrounding landscape.

above: site plan: the grade beams become a system for organizing the surrounding landscape; forming a sand pit, a low bench, and a walkway.

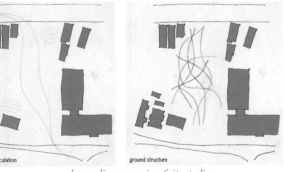

circulation   ground structure   building structure   skin + circulation   program

above: diagram series of site studies.

right: site model showing the school as structural intervention.

a high school for higher ground | cecilia hernandez nichols

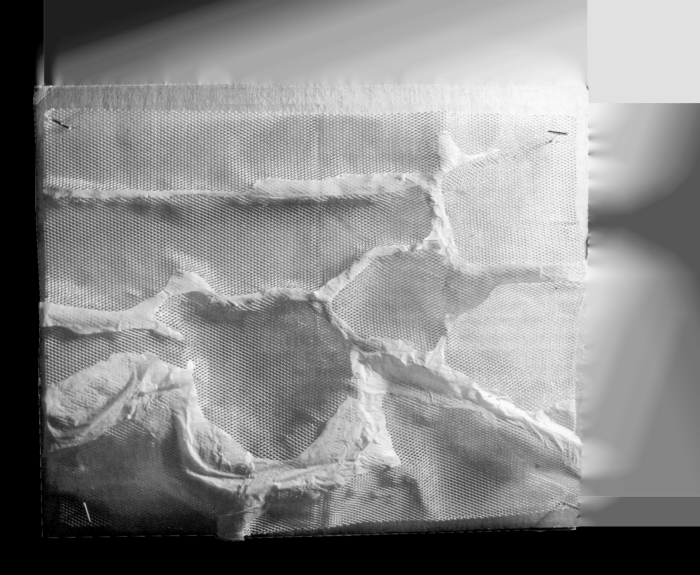

BUILDING AS A VERB

Our research at the University of Virginia over the past decade has focused on the reconstruction of public schools in devastated
tions as a vehicle for community action and consequential self-identity. My initial work in developing third world nations commer
my Peace Corps experience with John Turner and Peter Land in Peru 1967-69, resulting in school guidelines incorporated in the
Competition (1970). This initial experience identified three strategic lessons tested in countless school projects transposed from A
to Lima onto sites in Houston/Richmond/Philadelphia and currently storm devastated New Orleans.

These critical lessons are pragmatic and self-evident.
Identify the economy of resources at hand
Promote the immediate empowerment of self-help projects
Strategize the utility of incremental development

Since the Boyer Report Building Community (1995) challenged architectural education to re-articulate the mission of schools,
collaborating with Stephen Bingler, we have sought to develop models from foundations to finishes that make immediately po
sultant consequences of weathering and the utility of fingerprints. We continue our focused research project now in collaboratio
members of the Tulane University's School of Architecture to develop Specifications for Construction for the Hynes Elementa
Neighborhood Center for the Lakeview District of New Orleans.

We identify strategies for rebuilding infrastructure at the urban scale as the foundation upon which to locate the school as r
new higher ground; to plan incremental strategies for renewing devastated terrains as remediation and resource, and to identify
materials, some call dirty waste as fecund resources to be used on site and not viewed as useless material to be hauled away. We
visible spatial tales of origin as specifications for construction to serve as Primers for Planning to Stay (Morrish). Local citizens a
to act now through self-help advocates as on-site Surveyors, Gardeners and Engineers in the face of the Nomadic condition whe

7

For millennia the human imagination has conceived of a series of climatic precincts to withstand and be weathered by the natural pre-conditions of the storm. Very few were designed to both survive yet be vulnerable enough to be rebuilt in part by every generation as an ethical condition of citizenship. Perhaps Noah had it right. Build a good tight ship in dry-dock; collect every manner of beast and a few perfect and imperfect strangers to amuse them, and develop a sense of patience and enduring optimism to ride out the storm. Humankind has been rebuilding the World, Again for sometime now. Mr. Jefferson's university might offer a Lesson or two on how to construct sites in the name of a topographic imagination.

ON SPECIFICATIONS FOR CONSTRUCTION/A SYNTAX OF STRUCTURE AT THE SCALES OF THE CLASSROOM AND THE CITY

The City of New Orleans has dedicated a massive relief effort over the next decade to reconsider and rebuild the physical facilities of places of lifetime learning and civic interaction for long-term residents and estranged newcomers as well. This studio will focus on the transformation of hydraulic situations of punctuated grid settlements to the east and the west, on a building site located at the edge of City Park with a turbulent river to the south and a massive lake to the north.

ON DOORS & WINDOWS/ATTICS & BASEMENTS/ AND ONE BLACKBOARD

We will commence with projections for one classroom with one door to enter and two to exit; two windows to mark the start and finish of the school day and one other to permit the Moon to trespass this heretofore familiar space. There will be a myriad (try 28) cubbies, but only one remarkable blackboard, with one basement to give dimension between floor and ground, and a correspondent attic to distinguish between ceiling and roof. We will alternate between an intimate classroom scale one week to follow responsively with the pre-conditions of the site at the scales of the massive hydraulic region, the city of neighborhoods, the city park and the thickened edge in between all these scales.

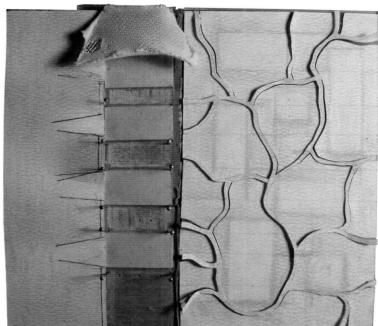

left: An exaggerated topographic map of New Orleans displays only the land area above sea level. by Lauren Shirley right: site strategy for urban block adjacent to canal addressing path, gathering, and topography by Lauren Shirley.

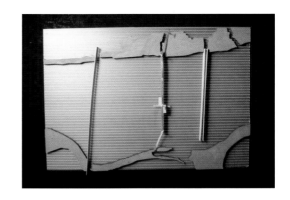

Swimming Instruction: Water, Sur la Tete and Underfoot
lauren shirley

This project began with the assumption that it is unacceptable and illegitimate to build on land below sea level. This was, of course, completely at odds with our non-negotiable site, which was situated in a neighborhood 9 feet below sea level. This project is based on the realization of a new public infrastructure, a bridge built along the top of an improved canal wall that would bridge the social and physical divide by connecting people from lower neighborhoods to areas of the city that are above sea level.

At our site, classrooms perch along the canal wall, allowing for outdoor learning space and a view of the fearsome water from a height of 20 feet. They are anchored in the city block, yet watchful of and interactive with the water and the park. Students and visitors enter the main part of the school on the north side of the block at the administrative building. The sequence of spaces continues south through the outdoor cafeteria, gymnasium and library, ending in a large covered auditorium/gathering space. Each space is laid out on raised plinths in the footprint of the flooded Hynes School. To the east and towards the canal, adjacent and to each of these spaces are indoor rooms with corresponding functions for hot or rainy weather. These are embanked in the earth as it slopes up to meet the top of the canal wall, and sit below a large undulating green roof that, at its dips, provides access to the roof and, at its peaks, provides access to the interior. Above, catwalks connect these spaces to the classrooms by the canal.

Freed up by moving most of the functions of the school towards the canal, more than half of the site is open to be used, at first, as a site for consolidating recovery efforts in the neighborhood, later as playing fields and community gardens, and, in inclement weather, as a floodplain. From this lowest level, to the raised plinths of the main structure, up to the classrooms atop the 20 foot canal wall, and perhaps later even further on across a bridge into the park, this project creates several vertical strata of paths and learning spaces designed to take on the reality of New Orleans' topography.

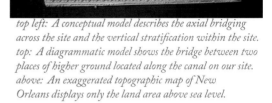

top left: A conceptual model describes the axial bridging across the site and the vertical stratification within the site.
top: A diagrammatic model shows the bridge between two places of higher ground located along the canal on our site.
above: An exaggerated topographic map of New Orleans displays only the land area above sea level.

below: The site plan and analysis illustrates two ways of bridging: one between the school and the park across the canal, and the other along the canal between points of higher ground.

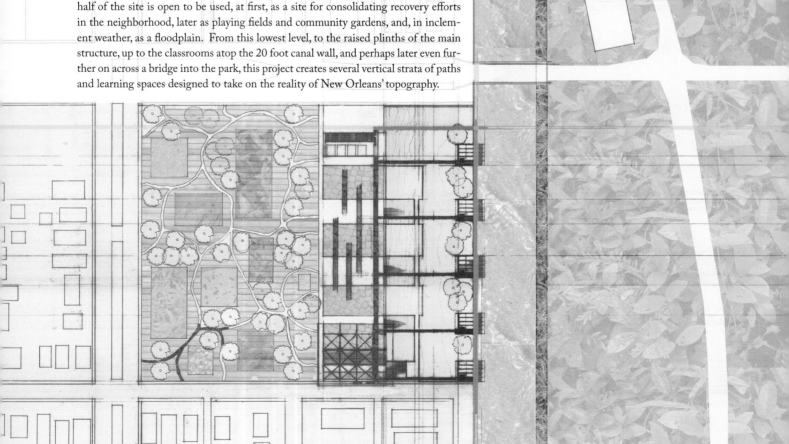

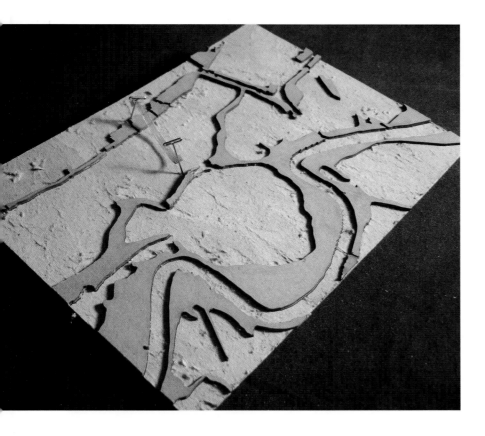

above: The model of the landscape scheme shows catwalks and indoor halls turn into meandering, raised paths that navigate a geometry of playing fields and gardens, wet or dry.

left: This analytical model of New Orleans shows the area above sea level. A bridge stretches over our site between two ridges of high ground.

below: A view shows the indoor gymnasium and green roof from outdoor playground and gathering space. Visible in the background are the catwalks that lead to the classrooms along the canal.

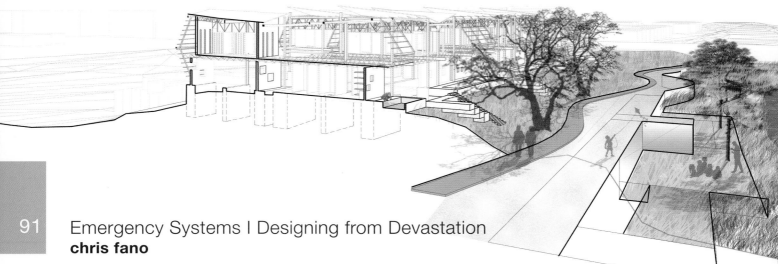

91

Emergency Systems I Designing from Devastation
chris fano

As a commentary on designing from devastation, New Orleans presents an interesting opportunity for reclamation, reinterpretation, and rejuvenation. By exploiting what is now a palette of forgotten materials, this project for a new elementary school in the Lakeview neighborhood explores the notion of reinvisioning the relationship New Orleans holds with its environment.

Through the development of earth levees and "green" corridors along canal edges, nature becomes a much more approachable and understood element of everyday life in the city. These green "fingers" would be programmed with a variety of infrastructural and recreational municipal services. The elementary school project would serve as such a moment where weather and natural processes merge with both design and curriculum. Animated wind screens, natural ventilation in classrooms, daylighting, active solar arrays, and stormwater management systems become active participants in the operation of the school, and serve to educate on how site and systems interact to define a sense of place.

below: top perspective: interior views shows a classroom module
lower perspective:: exterior perspective showing shade
screens to east that extend the space of the classroom

below: Sectional drawing shows stormwater conveyance
and collection that integrates school and site systems.

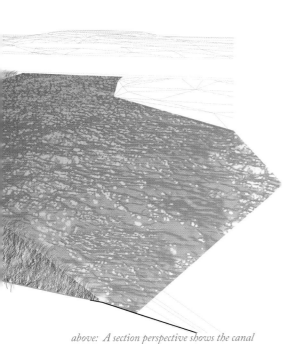

above: A section perspective shows the canal edge becoming a riparian corridor; a zone for recreation, rehabilitation, and education.

above: Site model shows the extension of school curriculum to weather centers situated along the canal.

above: exterior perspective showing west facade of elementary school complex

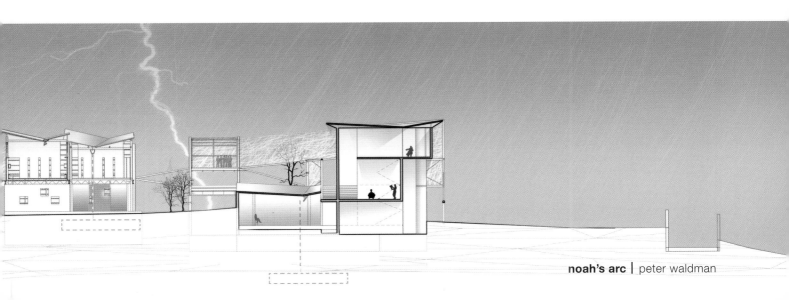

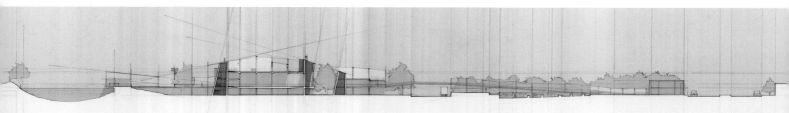

*above: longitudinal site section through
main community spaces*

93 Twofold Fields I Regenerating the Site and Sense of Community
tina cheng

The Hynes Elementary School is envisioned as the heart of the community where the site strategy is a cyclical, divided field. One half of the site is left fallow and used as a resource center where building materials can be brought on site by eighteen wheelers and barges and stored as reconstruction takes place in the surrounding Lakeview neighborhood and in greater New Orleans. In contrast, the cultivated side becomes a source of income and work as the community grows cayenne pepper, scallions, and bay leaves that will be sold in a farmers market.

Every two years, the functions of the two halves are inverted cyclically. The curriculum of the school also reflects the site strategy, where the younger grades learn about agriculture and the older grades use the surrounding infrastructure systems such as the proposed Bridgekeeper's gate and a series of new canal locks as the basis for their education.

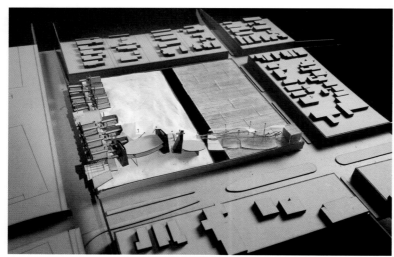

left: site model

below: Sectional drawing through the Great room shows active/congregational space (gym, cafeteria, auditorium) and passive space (reading room).

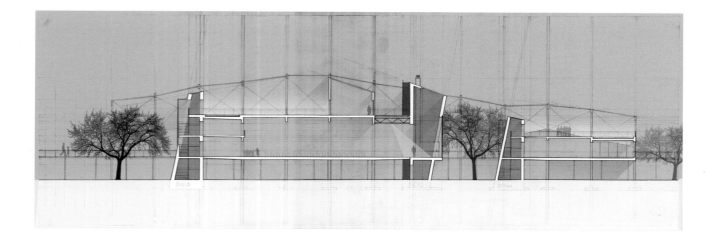

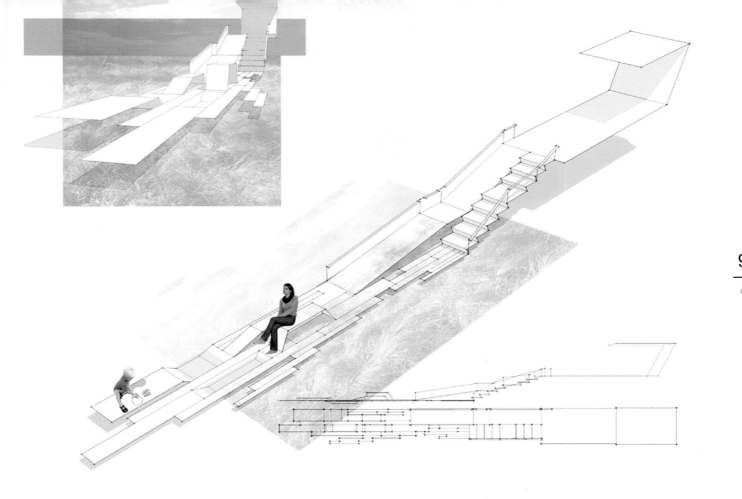

above: explorations in paths leading up to the classrooms
below: transverse section through the great room

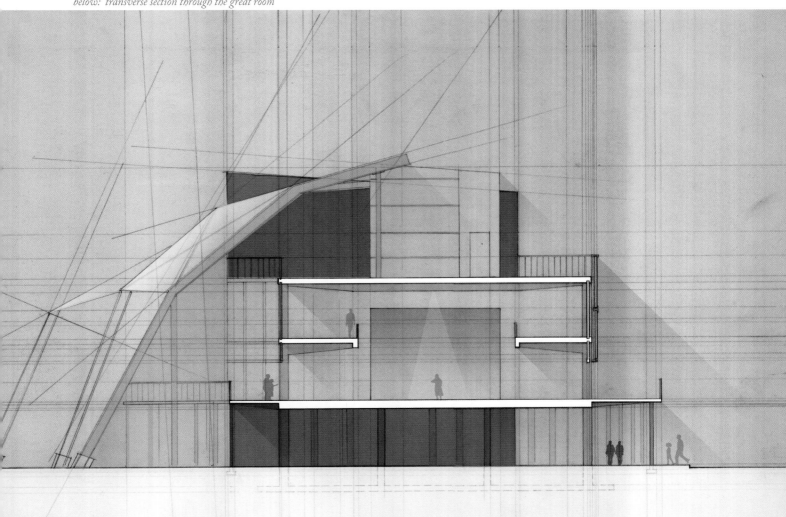

noah's arc | peter waldman

95

Twofold Fields I Regenerating the Site and Sense of Community
tina cheng

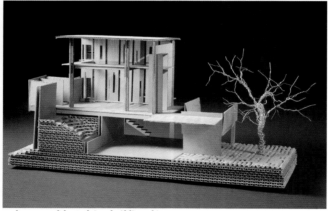

above: models studying building skins and connections to the ground.

below: transverse site section through great room with classroom elevations beyond transverse site section

above and below: sectional perspectives studying materials and connections

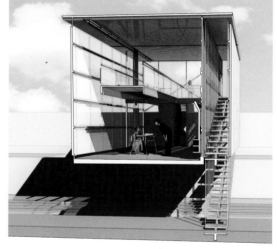

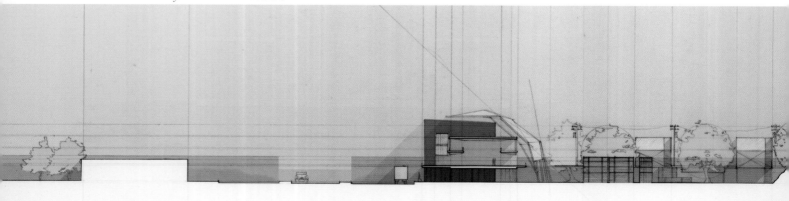

7

below: site plan: This scheme situates the elementary school and community space programs onto the canal and north edges of the site, and uses the expanse of the site as a strategy for construction and collection of building resources.

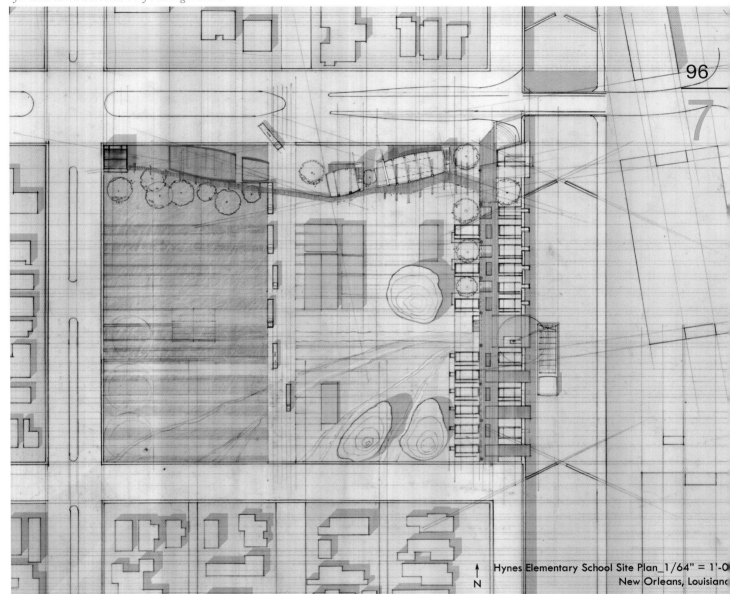

↑
N
Hynes Elementary School Site Plan_1/64" = 1'-0
New Orleans, Louisiana

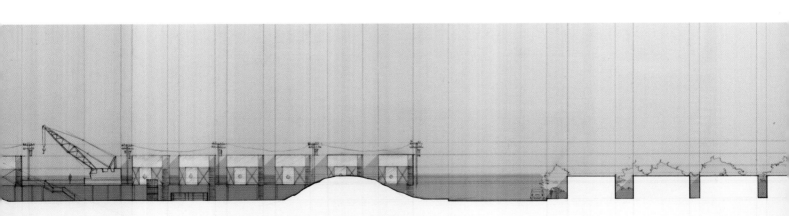

noah's arc | peter waldman

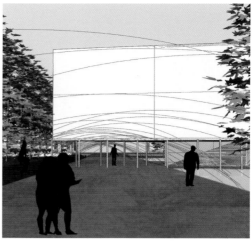

Edward Hynes Elementary School
Letting go, Picking up, and Going on
corey barnes

The design for the new Edward Hynes Elementary School provided both a chance for the community to come together for the common cause of their children and also a chance to create a building that was integrally tied to its climatic context. The dichotomy between the strong and heavy concrete walls and the light canopied areas provides both a point around which to rebuild after a time of crisis, but also a common project for the community every time the area is hit by a major storm.

The concrete walls are meant to weather the storm; resistant to mold and flooding, they will be the anchors around which the school is built after the next storm. The canopied areas are meant to be washed and blown away with the water and wind, yet will subsequently be rebuilt by the community, giving them a rendezvous point and common project around which to begin anew.

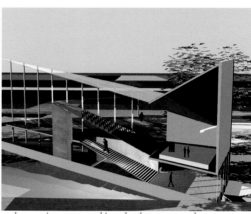

above: views approaching the classrooms and sectional perspective of the auditorium

left: sectional perspective of the classrooms

97

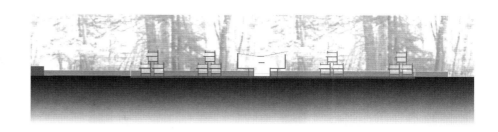

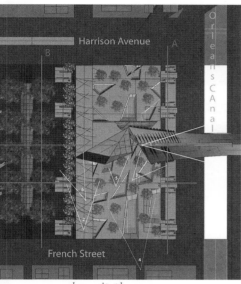

above: site plan

above: section cuts taken through the site

below: Sectional perspective drawings show the library and classroom spaces.

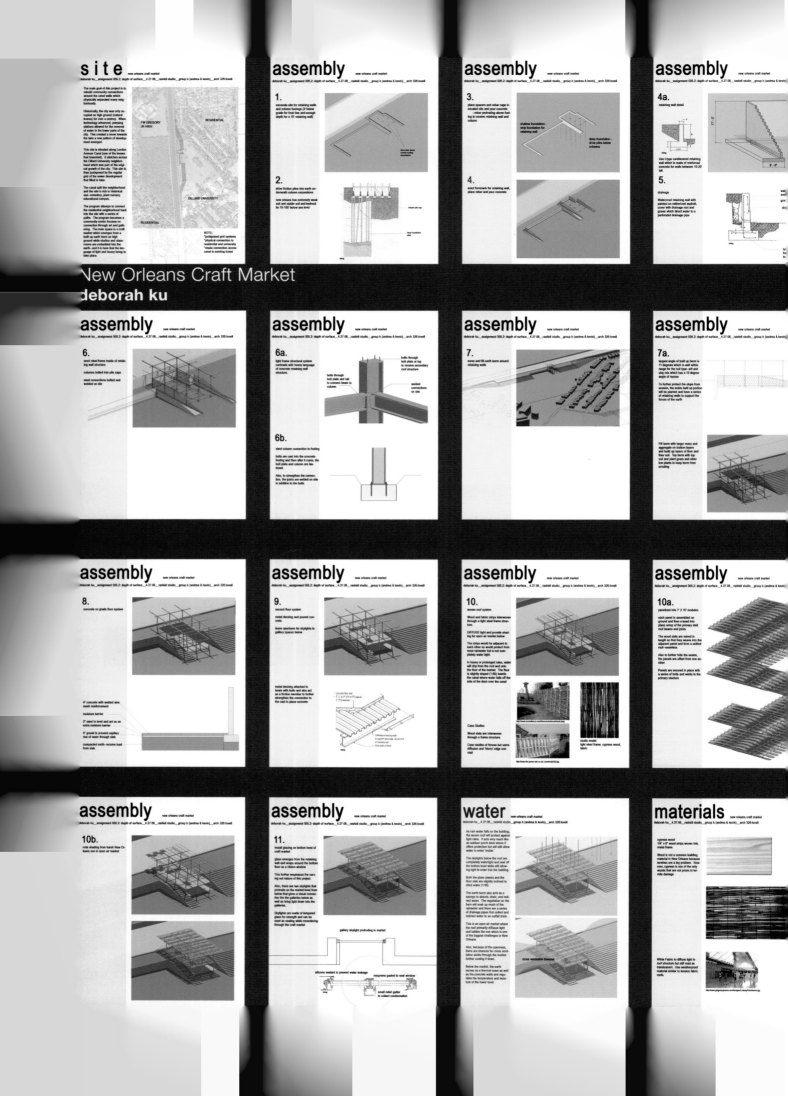

New Orleans Craft Market
deborah ku

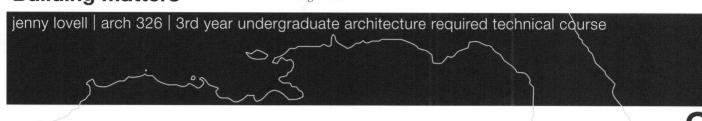

Long before Katrina struck New Orleans, warnings of rising water levels and stormy weather, as a result of global warming, were widely circulated.[1] This shift in expected seasonal weather ranges and our changing relationship to water requires a re-evaluation of systems of structure, building environment and building envelope that must be adopted. Building assemblies that previously have been accepted as a vernacular 'solution' perhaps are now not appropriate due to their inability to withstand the increasingly more aggressive force of water from the sky and the ground.

8

The third year studios with projects set in New Orleans during spring 2006 were forced to engage poignant issues of inside and outside, of above and below. How does the designer address structure and envelope without implying a sense of impending doom? The work shown within this essay exemplifies ways in which students were encouraged to 'unpack' their projects in terms of a sequence of assembly and to diagram how materials are connected rather than approaching design as purely 'object' making.

'Building Matters' (ARCH 326) is the course that introduces undergraduates to construction. The syllabus focuses on basic building principles, techniques, materials, and the relationship between envelope and structure. Construction principles are reviewed from the perspective of poetic intent and the necessity for pragmatic responses to the complex issues of site, context, and program. These two approaches are not set out as a binary or opposing condition, but rather as part of an overall and holistic solution to place and program which privileges balance over deterrence.

A constant thread that weaves through the course is how to address 'water' at all scales of construction: 'breathability', drainage and potential ingress from seasonal condition to extreme environment. Students are asked: What is the intention behind the way your building meets the ground, and touches the sky? Where does rainwater go? Where is the weather line? How is water managed? How is the envelope allowed to breathe and fluctuate? From tolerance of construction, assembly, and differential movement to changes in weather and climate - nothing is static.

The first half of the semester explores key principles of construction from the ground to the sky (not necessarily in that order) with an overview of systems: load-bearing walls, frames and combinations thereof. Each system is reviewed by looking at a series of case studies that articulate both the 'typical' and the extra-ordinary condition. The second half of the semester examines building materials and envelope and the 'ambiguity between the building as frame, and the building as wall' to gain an understanding of materials, systems, and intersections - and why one might be pursued over another in a specific design response, above and beyond necessity.

In the course of the semester, students are issued five assignments that align with lectures, workshops and readings. Assignments 001 through 004 utilize case studies and scenarios as a means to explore specific assemblies or elements; foundations, roof, frame, wall, and envelope. The final assignment, those shown here, ask students to consider their own studio project through the appropriate lenses that have been established in each of the previous assignments.

This open air craft market was about the community and reconnecting a 'broken' neighborhood. Issues of water were of immediate concern because this is the canal that breached during Hurricane Katrina. In order to manage water, the roof of the main structure is a light steel frame with thin cypress planks woven through it. This provides protection during light rain storms and allows water to filter through and run into the canal during heavy storms. The structure of the building and the earth berm act as secondary supports to the canal wall. The weight and force of the earth would further enforce the strength of the wall and also allow for the wall system to become occupiable.

1 For example: National Geographic October 2004 as referred to by Edward Mazria AIA 'Resuscitating a Dying World' for 2010imperative.org

2 Bob Allies & Graham Morrison 'A Particular Point of View' in Michigan Papers: 1996.

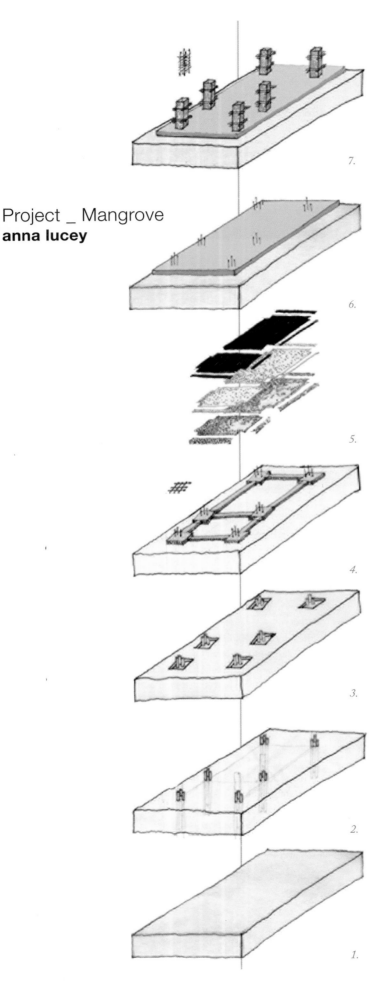

Project _ Mangrove
anna lucey

Project Mangrove is a preschool in the city of New Orleans, located on the knuckle of St. John's Bayou. The site is a unique crossroads of historically significant buildings, pre-existing schools, and topographic features (namely the ridge that runs through the north of the site). The design addresses the delicate balance between earth, water, and sky.

1. Ground Condition: on a ridge in New Orleans, 8 ft. above sea level.

2. Piles: driven into the earth until in contact with stable ground. They are grouped in threes and will eventually be the foundation for load-bearing columns.

3. Excavation: areas around the piles are excavated. The earth is typically held back with temporary wood shoring.

4. Pile Caps: The pile caps are connected by grade beams to give the structure unity and stability.

5. Gravel/ sand/ damp proof membrane.

6. Concrete Slab: a concrete slab is poured, edges are supported by temporary wood formwork. Vertical reinforcement protrudes for later connection to the poured in place concrete columns.

7. Columns formwork: temporary formwork is erected of plywood sheet and 2"x4". Concrete is poured inside and around a rebar cage.

8. The concrete columns set.

9. The column formwork is stripped off and, in preparation for the addition of the roof, weatherproofing is added to the sides of the columns that will face the exterior. Roof Truss: steel connections are fixed to the columns for the prefabricated wood trusses (comprised of 2"x6"). Bearing steel plates are added to truss joints for reinforcement. The plates are attached using through-bolts (from one side of the truss to another) and anchor bolts from the steel plates to the reinforced concrete columns. The trusses span 16 ft.o.c.

10. Purlins & Roof Layers: the distance from one truss to another is spanned by purlins at 16" o.c. Next, 4 ft. x 8 ft. plywood acts as the roof decking. 4 ft. x 8 ft. panels of rigid foam insulation are then nailed to the decking. Above that is the waterproofing layer of the roof build-up. On top of this rests a wear course of gravel which protects the membrane and acts as ballast. The final finish is copper sheet metal with standing seams at 24" o.c.

11. Interior Flooring: after the heavy-duty work is over (and dirty work boots are no longer a constant presence), the delicate flooring is installed. The first layer is 1" of screed. Laid on this are terrazzo tiles 1 ft x 1 ft.

12. Inside/Outside: the wall separating the classroom from the outdoor space consists of panels of frosted glass in laminated 4 ft. x 10 ft. units. Their joints are sealed with preformed glazing tape. The interior walls are a simple timber-frame construction, sealed to the reinforced concrete columns with a thin layer of building felt to minimize temperature transfer.

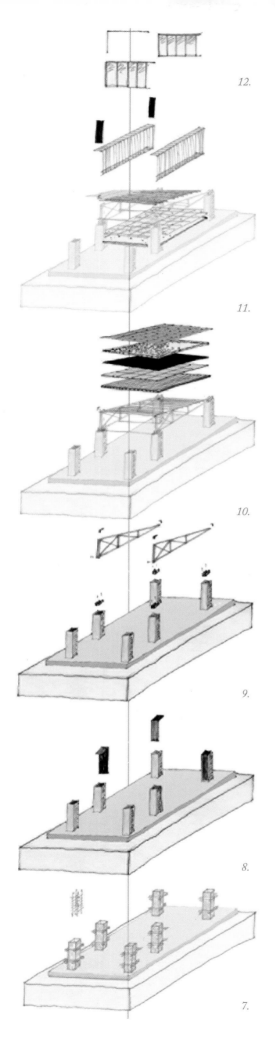

12.

11.

10.

9.

8.

7.

'underground: overground'
assignment 001

The intention behind assignment 001 was to consider the way the building meets the ground in a given example. Students constructed three-dimensional digital models articulating every step of the building sequence on site.

In class, we looked at the intention behind how a building might 'touch the ground' together with the pragmatic requirements of footing and foundations details. For this exercise, students worked in pairs to review a given foundation detail.

Each pair was issued with a different detail from current journals. Rather than seeing the drawing as an object and a confusion of adjacencies, the charge was to start to re-present the details in terms of a sequence of construction and to diagram how materials are connected. What is the first construction activity that needs to be carried out here? What are the subsequent activities up to and including the connection with the superstructure? All the example details had to meet the same basic requirements: support, connection, transfer, waterproofing, drainage, and insulation – but all had different aesthetic implications borne out of a specific context.

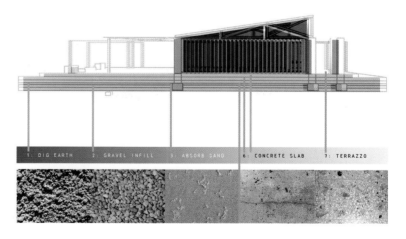

1: DIG EARTH   2: GRAVEL INFILL   3: ABSORB SAND   6: CONCRETE SLAB   7: TERRAZZO

103

Twofold Fields
Regenerating the Site and Sense of Community
tina cheng

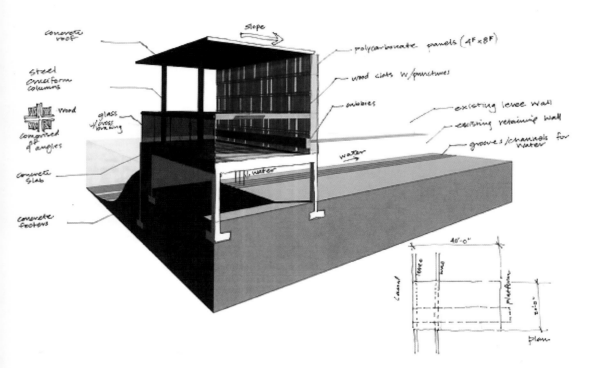

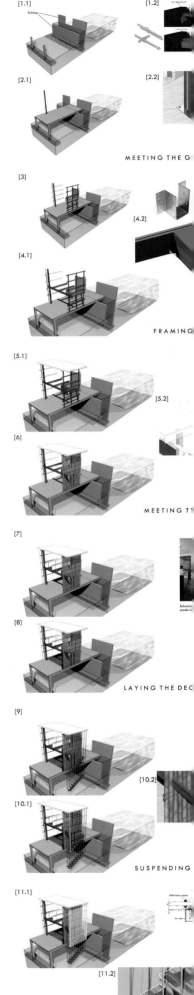

In response to Hurricane Katrina, the proposed classrooms
for Hynes Elementary School were designed to integrate
strategies that can minimize damage from future storms
and to create a space conducive to learning through thermal
comfort, natural ventilation, shading, and natural
daylighting.

The classrooms are buttressed against the levee wall to provide
structural reinforcement against the pressure of canal water.

The main floor of the classrooms is elevated off
the ground to reduce future flood damage.

Each classroom sits on concrete piers on a
cast-in-place strip foundation.

The southern façade is comprised of wooden components
recycled from the formwork used to cast the foundation.

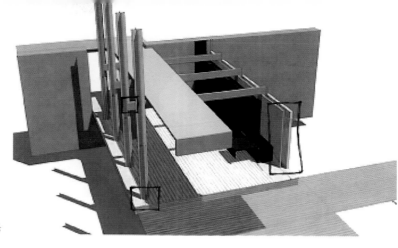

These recycled wood slats shade the interior of the classroom and are protected by a layer of operable polycarbonate panels that are supported by the slight cantilever of the metal decking roof. The roof extends past this polycarbonate panel wall so that rainwater falls away from the structure and is collected in channels below. The polycarbonate wall further functions as a rainscreen and a gap is left at the top to allow heat to dissipate on the exterior side of the classroom.

The northern wall is comprised of only polycarbonate panels to allow indirect northern light. To support the roof, cruciform columns are made from two extruded angles with wood pieces to flesh out the volume to a square section. They rest on a base plate to distribute the concentrated loads. The beams that support the catwalk double up to connect either side of the cruciform columns.

The objective of assignment 002 was to consider the overall massing and roof form of a building and how it meets the ground. Where and how are connections between sky and earth made in terms of water?

In considering both the ground and the roof, it was recognized that the two are inextricably linked. Designing in a linear progression from the ground up is not an option; a design strategy that addresses and coordinates both must be developed. For assignment 002, and again working in pairs, students were issued with a different case study, this time to investigate the roof assembly and the rainwater strategy for the building and adjacent site. How does the form of the roof shed water – and where to? What is the rainwater system and where are the outlets? What is the material build-up of the roof as a fifth elevation? How does this material choice relate to the overall building strategies and aesthetic? How does the building meet the sky?

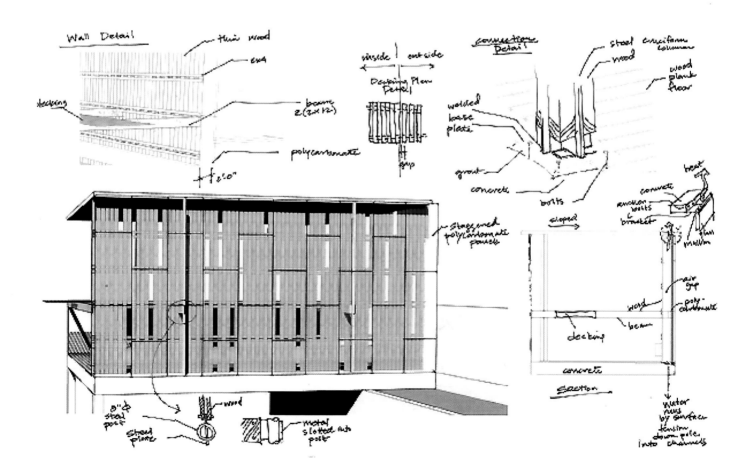

Emergency Systems I Designing from Devastation
chris fano

As a commentary on designing from devastation, New Orleans presents an interesting opportunity for material reclamation, reinterpretation, and rejuvenation. In addition to incorporating climatic and natural processes into the design narrative, this project for a new elementary school in the Lakeview neighborhood attempts to explore the potential of this new palette of disgarded materials. The oxidized steel members and concrete slabs, for example, were to be reclaimed from the framework of the existing school that currently occupies the site. Although not all materials are viable, the act of reusing alludes to both a sense of preservation and adaptation to catastrophic change. New materials, such as Building Integrated Photovoltaic Shingles, would reinforce a new sustainable agenda, and begin to define a boundary between old and new construction.

In addition to material reclamation, the project explores a larger idea of re-envisioning the relationship New Orleans holds with its environment. Through the development of earth levees and "green" corridors along the canal edge, nature becomes a much more approachable and understood element of everyday life in the city. The elementary school project reinforces this agenda, for weather and natural processes are integral to both design and curriculum. Animated wind screens, naturally ventilated classrooms, daylighting, adjustable brise-soleil, and stormwater management systems become active participants in the operation of the school, and serve to educate how site and systems interact to define a sense of place.

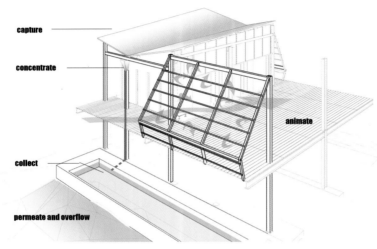

Natural Ventilation oriented to prevailing winds

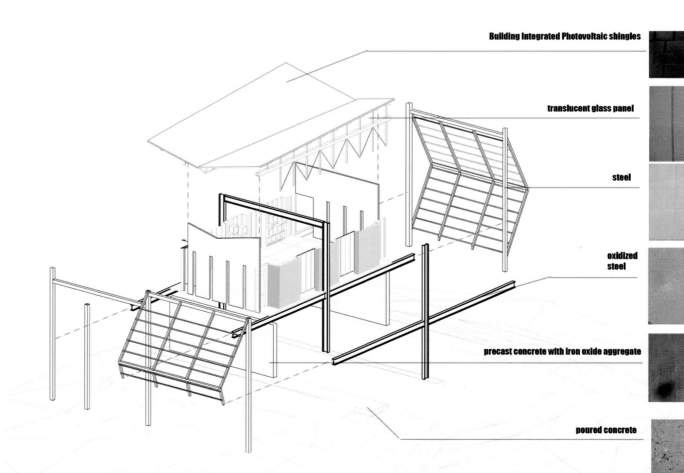

Building Integrated Photovoltaic shingles

translucent glass panel

steel

oxidized steel

precast concrete with iron oxide aggregate

poured concrete

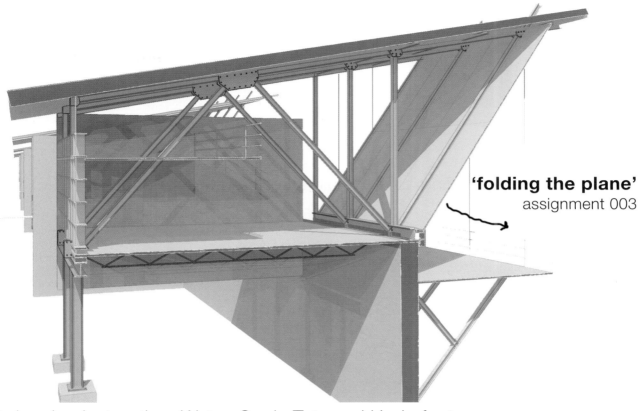

Swimming Instruction: Water, Sur la Tete and Underfoot
lauren shirley

Classrooms perch on top of the canal wall, grounded in the earth, yet watchful of, and curious about, the water. Each classroom has a dry area and a wet area that plugs into a raised walkway along the canal, a proposed piece of social infrastructure.

Three full height concrete walls are poured on strip foundations, one on either side of the classroom and one more offset from the south side, and support the floor. The two walls on the south side form the exterior entrance to the classroom and the entrance to the raised walkway yet also distinguish between them.

Caissons on one side and the canal wall on the other are used as foundations for three full height trusses that support the roof and form the frame for the windows and chalkboards along the east canal façade. These can open to include the 'wet' area that overhangs the canal in the classroom, or close to stay dry.

On the opposite facade, facing west and towards the rest of the school, is a 'thick' wall that functions as storage and as a brise-soleil. During the day, the back-packs and coats stored in the thick wall contribute to the amount of shade it provides. A series of small clerestories on this wall not only provides ventilation, but emphasizes the detachment of the roof from the heavy concrete walls.

The roof is clad with tiles that provide thermal mass to delay heat absorption during the day and release it at night. Each unit functions as an independent classroom for one grade level while connections to other classrooms occur in a realm of discovery.

Assignment 003 was directed at understanding structural systems, namely the load-bearing wall, and how to make aperture and 'turn' corners. Students considered one given system of wall construction: English bond brick bearing wall, Concrete Masonry Unit (CMU) bearing wall, cavity wall (running bond brick outer wythe and inner CMU wythe), tilt up concrete slab wall or 'fair faced' cast in place concrete wall.

The objective of this assignment was to consider how a structural system and the unit of a material or fabrication can be utilized to convey the building's design intention.

In terms of the New Orleans studios, walls often became the 'backbone' of a scheme. The wall was considered as an organizing structure not just in terms of support but also for the program and as a potential 'remnant' from which, should disaster strike, a place could be rebuilt.

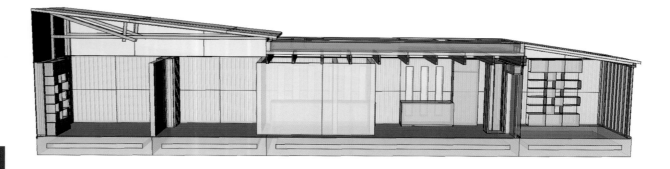

107

New Orleans I Rebuilding as a Sustainable Community
sheena mayfield

The rebuilding of New Orleans offers great potential to address the issues of designing for disaster-struck cities. Hurricanes and flooding are re-occurring events and must be planned for in a proactive manner recognizing that nature will find a way over or around 'fixed' barriers. New construction should be able to shift and negotiate flooding without being destroyed by the water, or mold in the aftermath. Intense sunlight, heat, and humidity are also constant issues in the delta region. Any new design should take into account this fact and produce structures which can be kept comfortable in an affordable manner. This means relying on passive design with mechanical systems used only as a back-up. In addition to the subtropical climatic factors, the rebuilding of New Orleans must take into consideration the socioeconomic situation of the people who are most affected by disasters such as Katrina. As the architect and psychologist Roberta Feldman stated, "Maybe we should be questioning why we're not building houses the way we build cars." With a mass-produced system, areas prone to flooding can be re-built, after a disaster, in an economically viable way and in a sustainable manner. Composite materials, or resources like bamboo that grow quickly, can be used to maximize building lifespan and minimize impact on limited resources. If the buildings' design also minimizes damage during a disaster, then more natural and economic resources are saved because re-building would be less costly after the next storm, allowing people to return to their homes more swiftly.

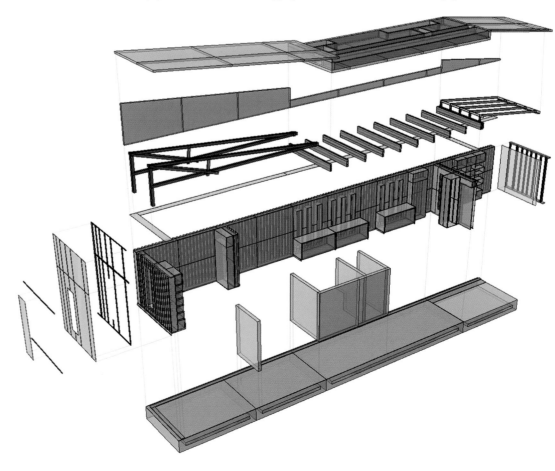

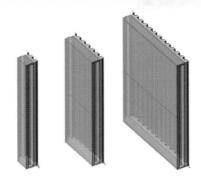

Standard Modules in three sizes: 6 ft., 3 ft. and 1 ft.

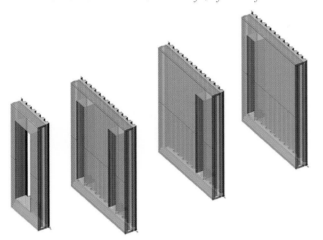

Window Modules

Light wood frame can be construed as a part wall / part frame system. Similarly to the previous exercise, assignment 004 asked students to explore the light wood frame system as a highly standardized yet ultimately flexible structural solution. Each pair had to make an enclosure from a 150 ft. external length with 4 to 8 possible corners, 9 apertures and 2 thresholds.

The possibility of the frame system and the ease with which it can be constructed was soon realized. The combination of a wall and a frame allowed staged development and the potential for prefabrication of components that could then be assembled quickly on site with a small and even a relatively inexperienced workforce. 'Habit for Humanity' has long realized the power of a willing pair of hands with directed access to a hammer and nails.

Program Modules: shelves, threshold, counter, closet

Wall Layers, the kit of parts

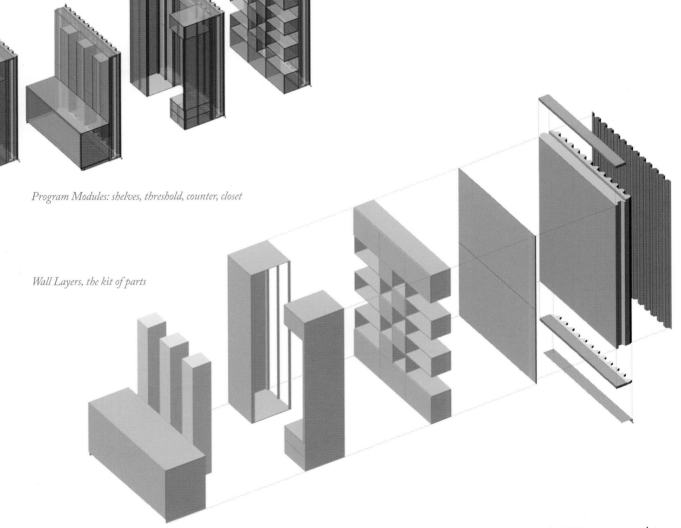

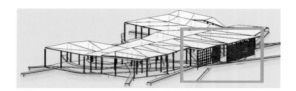

Beams connect columns

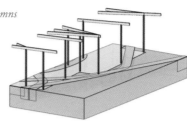

109

Pathways Preschool
sarah ramsey

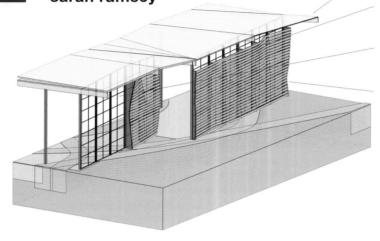

*Glazing system is installed
flush with roof and columns*

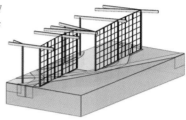

*Vertical mullions with
varying profiles are attached
onto the glazing system
to create the sun screen.*

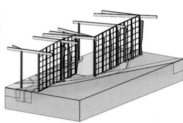

*Wooden planks are attached
to the mullions creating a sun
screen with a dynamic profile.*

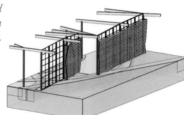

The ground in New Orleans is notoriously difficult to
build on. The soil is silty and swampy, causing buildings
to sink over time. Many buildings in New Orleans are
built using a simple slab-on-grade foundation; however,
this building technique hardly solves problems of settlement. Even worse, in flood conditions many of these
simple foundations cause buildings to 'detach' from their
site because they lacked a solid connection to the ground.
By creating a foundation system that securely anchors a
building to the ground, both of these common problems
native to building in New Orleans can be solved...

*Rafters span between the
beams to strengthen the roof
and allow it to be sheathed.*

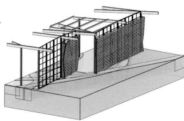

The proposed foundation system for this project uses both
piles and post-tensioned grade beams. This interlocking
system not only anchors the building to its site but also
strengthens the ground it locks into. The dialogue of this
two-foundation system is evident throughout the completed building, creating a didactic site for the building's
program, a nursery school.

The network of grade beams is flush with the floor slab
through which classrooms and hallways wind themselves,
representing the various paths a child is allowed to take
in a Montessori learning environment. The grade beams
extend beyond the floor slab to shape the landscape
surrounding the school; forming a bench, a sand pit, or
a walkway. The concrete columns supporting the roof of
the school are at various heights creating a contoured roof
plane intended to reflect the different depths that the
piles extend down into the ground. These contours help
to channel rainwater before eventually collecting it into a
central gutter down the spine of the building's roof.

*The roofing system is
built up on the rafters.*

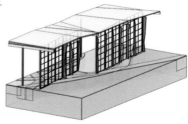

Hynes Elementary School
taryn harunah

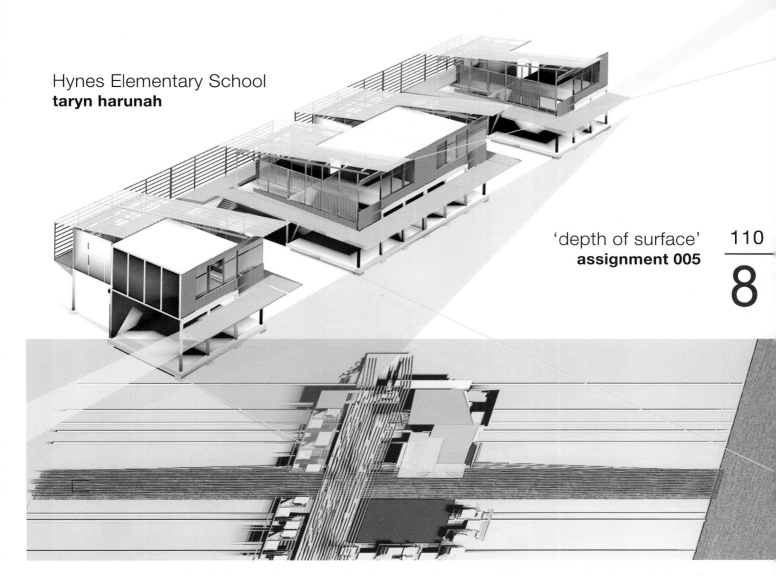

'depth of surface'   110
assignment 005

—

8

Assignment 005 'Depth of Surface' asked students to consider their own studio project with the intention of exploring the ideas of construction sequence, material deployment and assembly. The following questions were queried and researched through their design intentions.

Structure & Skin:
What is the relationship between structure and skin in the project; is a load-bearing wall or frame structural system proposed – or a combination of the two? What is primary, what is secondary in structural terms?

What is the intention behind the way the building meets the ground and the sky: Where does rainwater go? Where is the weather line? How is water managed? How is the envelope insulated?

Material:
What is the primary envelope material and why? What are its properties, how thick, how strong? How is it made? Is this a new building material application? What dimension is it fabricated at and what size is it as used in this application? How is it specific to this building? What is the context of the material?

Assembly:
What is the sequence of construction, where and how are things made and put together? How might they be re-constructed?

Above all construction, assembly, and materials should be considered as part of the context of place, idea, and solution. Those that visited New Orleans during this semester (or even those of us that tried to understand the devastation through images) became acutely aware of how relevant and essential the issues of the ARCH 326 Building Matters course are to re-making neighborhoods and a city, and how precious the resources are that enable that re-construction.

How a building meets the sky and how it touches the ground are much larger questions that need to work with, and not against, the environment – this is the generation of architects who undoubtedly have to address global issues through building.

JUSTIN & KATHLEEN EPISODIC

seeking higher density on higher ground

maurice cox | alar 702/802 | 2nd and 3rd year architecture and landscape arch graduate studio

9

BEN & JEREMY
DAILY/NIGHTLY

EL Maurice
ARCH 702 / 802

ALLI & JAMES
COLLISION

EL Maurice
ARCH 702 / 802

PATRICIA & HAO
IMPASSE

EL Maurice
ARCH 702 / 802

KRISTIN & LORENZO
EFFICIENCY

The city of New Orleans will be rebuilt.

Yet many questions have frustrated the process: Which parts? Under what system of protection? According to whose rules? In this sea of political uncertainty, only a few things appear to be clear - that the New Orleans that emerges from the devastation of Hurricane Katrina, will be smaller, more dense and built on higher ground. This studio explored issues of building high-density, mixed-income and mixed-use housing in the historic Bywater neighborhood of New Orleans.

Architectural Record sponsored the "High Density on the High Ground" competition in partnership with Tulane University's School of Architecture. We participated in order to contribute to the rebuilding of New Orleans by offering realistic yet innovative contemporary models for housing.

The program called for 140 units of housing, with a component of mixed use space and parking, on a about an acre and a half. These projects share a goal of being transformative while maintaining the city's unique cultural identity. Following the competition, the students were able to further develop their schemes individually to push their tectonic and sustainable building strategies.

The students worked collaboratively in pairs. In the beginning of the semester, we took a journey of learning to New Orleans. This trip provided an opportunity for students to "be in the present" as the human story of how people survive trauma and reconstruct their lives and homes unfolded. They were able to meet residents, gather stories, and explore how these stories might shape neighborhoods. In addition, they assisted several families in clearing out their damaged homes.

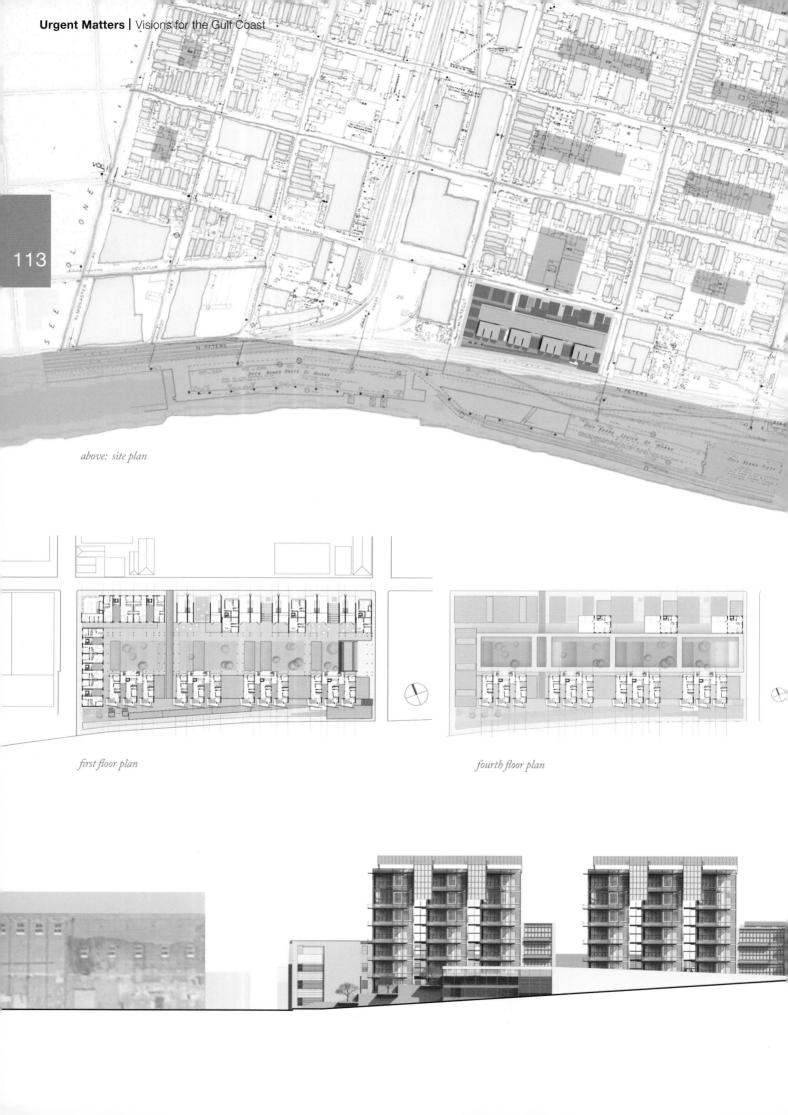

above: site plan

first floor plan

fourth floor plan

Neighborhood_River_Place
justin laskin + kathleen mark

Mediation of scale lies at the heart of understanding this site. The Bywater neighborhood's eclectic collision of industrial and residential scale establishes its unique character and identity. By mixing use and density within a former industrial swath, this proposal responds to the scale of the neighborhood and the river, the warehouse and the house, the body and its place.

The city block is lifted a story above street level and terraced both towards the river and the neighborhood. Parking is below, with easy connections to housing, retail, and community space. Off Chartres Street, a series of broad alleys connect the pedestrian to a new-elevated ground plane. This terracing alley becomes an informal performance space, fronting both the street and the court. The elevated court becomes a new gathering space with a market, restaurant/ café seating, and park. Affordable housing is interspersed throughout the entire city block, integrating size, location, and income level by providing a variety of unit configurations and orientations.

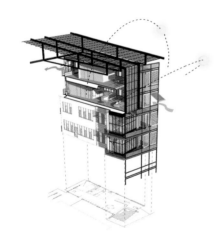

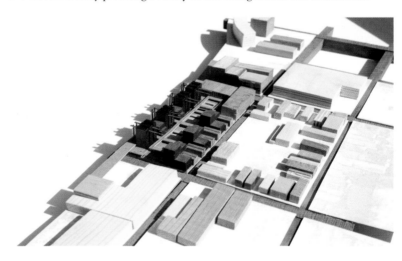

115

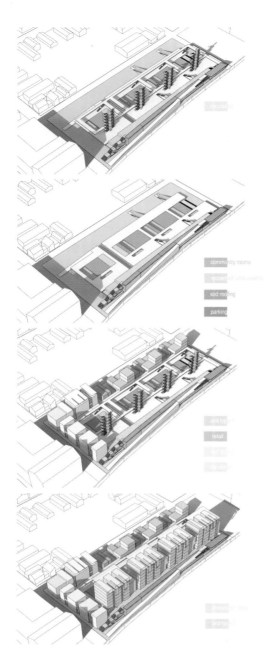

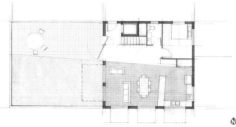

plan: housing unit 1

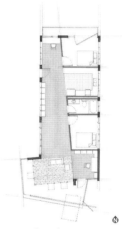

plan: housing unit 2

plan: housing unit 3

below: transverse site section

Neighborhood_River_Place
justin laskin + kathleen mark

A long ramp and step system lifts the back of the site to create a new river_view promenade. Arranged along the path are a series of community-gathering spaces, which lift from below to views of the river and downtown. This creates a strong sectional relationship between the passerby and the community. Above, outdoor gathering spaces and a community garden are shared with the neighboring tower units. Reclaimed brick pavers from the existing site become new paths. These paths extend beyond the block into the new internal courtyard, with connections west to NOCA and housing to the north.

The west edge of the site is a second housing type, with a new city center occupying the corner. Its apertures and massing respond to the Rice Mill façade, but interior courtyards break up its volume, giving each unity direct access to the outdoors.

Retail is located along Chartres Street; each unit is given a "corner store" location, a building type familiar to New Orleans. Housing Type 1 also has frontage along Charters Street, with street side and courtside balconies mediating the scale of the street and new internal court. Terraced massing achieves medium density configuration that can relate to the residential scale of the existing fabric it faces while providing roof gardens for housing.

Along the river's edge are a series of high-density towers, extensions of the natural levee. A third housing type comprises three distinct masses within each tower. This allows for light and air conditions to each exterior wall as well as outdoor space for every unit. Operable louver screens and balconies line the south face, blocking the harsh summer sun while still allowing river breezes to penetrate through the units and into the courtyards beyond. The direct exposure offered by the open river provides an ideal location for photovoltaic roof cells. While initial costs are high, the energy savings provided through natural ventilation and self-generated power would defray the costs of construction and help the complex remain affordable. Rainwater is collected from the roofs and piped to a cistern located on the first level, which is then used to water the gardens above.

This project was selected in the commended category — recognized as one of the top five entrants.

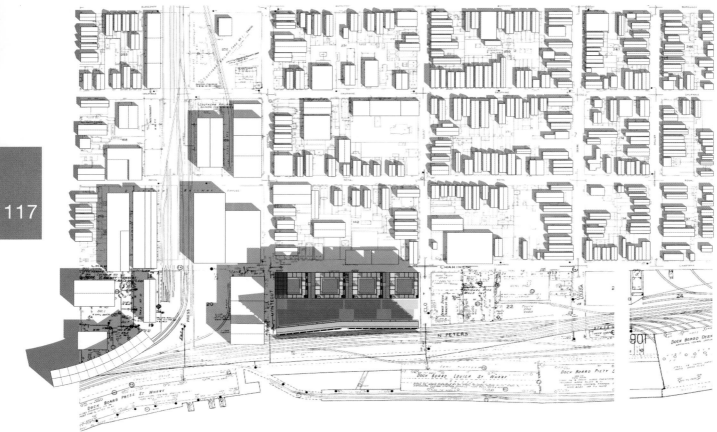

above: site plan showing neighborhood context
below: sectional perspective through the site

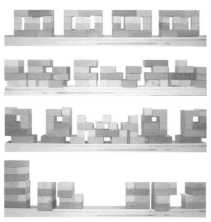
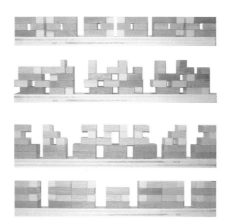

above: iterative study models of programmatic fit

"the work is hard – every shovel load heavy from being soaked. The process is simple – scrape it all up, shovel it into the wheel barrow, walk it outside, and dump it on the lawn next to the sidewalk. Some of the items are everyday things – couches, desks, filing cabinets, a piano, lamps, and kitchenware. Then there are personal items – files, correspondence, pictures, books, and clothing. I soon begin to recognize the reality and the immediate impact Katrina left on the lives of people. Not just houses, but lives have been gutted, and here I am rummaging through personal things, smashing apart a beautiful piano, and ripping down walls. I sit down in the middle of the street and view the house I just helped clear, mesmerized by the solemn stillness of the neighborhood. Like the weight and burden of the belongings I helped discard, my heart is heavy too."

This is the reality in New Orleans following Hurricane Katrina. For most people, returning to the city to salvage homes and re-establish lives is not only undesirable, but in some cases impractical. It is apparent that any new housing proposal for the revitalization of New Orleans must strive to re-establish the city's population. When people believe there is a reason to return, and that New Orleans is still a desirable place to live, only then can the discussion turn toward more effective methods of inhabitation.

Our proposal for the Bywater neighborhood incorporates a process of recovery and a process of renewal that simultaneously meet the immediate and long-term needs of the citizens. We envision an affordable housing process that provides temporary aid to the city through its various stages of construction, while maintaining a suitable living environment for families who are ready to reestablish their lives.

The project equally utilizes themes of standardization and individualization. While these concepts may at first appear to be conflicting, we feel that the housing typology in New Orleans is a good example of how the two can actually strengthen each other through their co-existence. New Orleans has a large housing stock of both "shotgun" and Creole "cottage" type dwellings, both of which are based on a particular form and style. However, a "standard" form and structure does not have to necessitate assembly line monotony, but rather provides a stable framework for an incredible variety of self-expression. The form takes care of the basic needs for living (space, ventilation, shade), while the occupants are free to customize the structure as desired.

Our project aspires to this goal with similar principles in mind. The modular system allows for ease of construction and aids in keeping project costs low, while the exposed faces of each unit allow and even require individual intervention. We envision the resulting tapestry of living units as rich and fulfilling with both an aesthetic and communal sensibility, maintaining the rich diversity that is New Orleans.

top above: study models of modules
above: sectional perspective

view the site approach from Chartres Street looking west

riverside view from the wharf area, soon to be a public park

view of the center court on the elevated ground plane looking west

view of the entrance to the site from Chartres Street up to the elevated ground plane

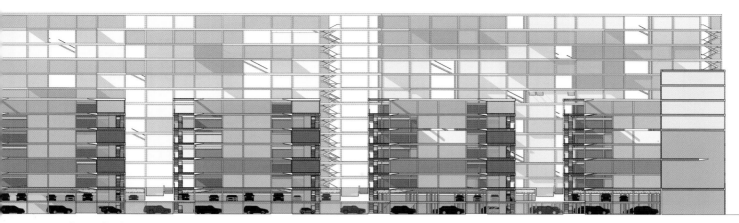

longitudinal section

Stage One: Grounding_Footprints and Disaster Relief

The first stage of the project consists of four large "warehouses" on Chartres Street. These structures will provide immediate space for the ongoing relief effort, and serve as a storage and meeting places for those involved in the recovery cycle. Simultaneously, the foundations will be laid for the column grid, which is to eventually support the entire structure. This grid will provide the organization for an open-air parking structure, and meet the needs of the site when it is built out to capacity.

Stage Two: "Higher Ground"_A Constructed Ground Plane

A new ground plane is established over the two-story parking structure, and temporarily serves as an elevated city park while the proposed public city park awaits completion. The ground comes down to meet Chartres Street in three places between the warehouse buildings. The undulating surface has three large fissures in section which allow light into the parking below. The ground place provides the base for the rest of the project, and meets a very practical need while speaking to a more metaphorical idea about future inhabitation within the city.

Stage Three: Possibilities_A Framework for Living

The structural concrete frame is erected within an established grid which provides the necessary syncopation for the flexible housing units which arrive in Stage 4. The frame contains vertical spaces for circulation and services, and a "trench" slab at each floor automatically provides spaces for utilities as the pre-fabricated units are installed. The integral balconies serve not only as circulation, but also provide a staging area for the light finish construction taken on by the first inhabitants of the space.

Stage Four: Return_RE-establishing a Population

The fourth stage involves the insertion of housing units in the frame. The units are pre-fabricated concrete cores which are structural and weatherproof, yet allow personal expression on the open faces. They are installed by a crane, and finish work is completed after the unit has already been placed. The units are arranged with bedroom "cores" which are connected by central living spaces in order to provide flexible living situations for the initial inhabitants who may be using the housing as a staging ground for more permanent re-inhabitation. Initial occupancy is devoted primarily to rental, with the possibility of shared units when the need or desire arises. The Tulane Center is also well underway at this stage, to provide a community design resource for the neighborhood and larger city.

Stage Five: Build Out_Project Completion

The completion of the project sees a well-established community thriving in New Orleans. Through the process of inhabitation, occupants will form bonds which will lead to a healthy, vibrant neighborhood. The major mode of occupancy is "rent to own" ownership, and residents have claimed their units as their own with countless examples of self-expression. The initial unit flexibility continues to be a major design feature, as the space requirements of ever-changing family dynamics are easily handled. The formative "warehouse" units now form a retail front on Chartres Street which encourages connection to the city of New Orleans on a larger scale. The completion of the Tulane Center insures that residents will continually have a voice in future work in and around their neighborhood, and on a metropolitan level as well.

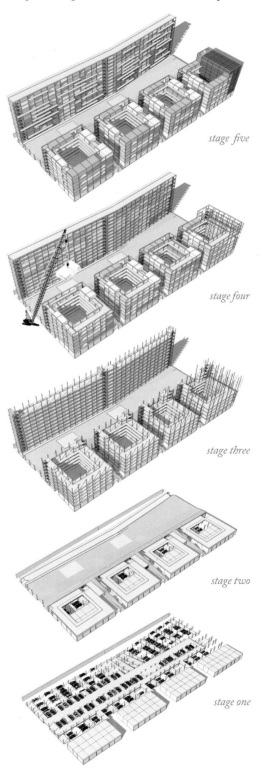

stage five

stage four

stage three

stage two

stage one

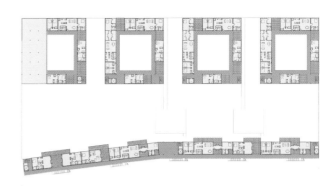

typical "higher ground" level floor plan

typical upper level floor plan

below: models studying outdoor and circulation spaces

*above: model showing pre-fabricated
units placed in framework
below: axon study of typical unit layout*

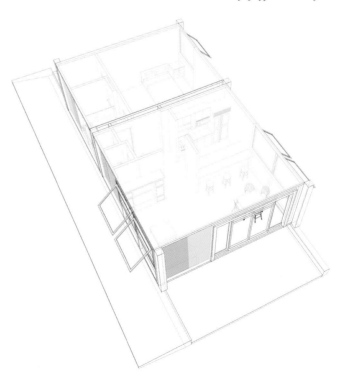

typical 1400 sf unit plan   typical 700 sf unit plan   typical 2100 sf unit plan

Return, Rebuild, Renew
jeremy kline + ben thompson

The Unit

The modular unit has a basic dimension of 20'x 35' for a total of 700 square feet. All units have a 20' cross dimension which allows generous cross-ventilation. The unit slides into the concrete framework, and is sheltered by the generous balcony overhangs from both the southern sun and the frequent heavy rains. Each unit has a large, private outdoor space, and is also joined to larger public gathering via circulation balconies. Larger units are arranged around the bedroom "pods", which will allow great flexibility during initial project construction and primary occupancy. This flexibility is invaluable in the ownership phase as well, as family dynamics constantly shift and change.

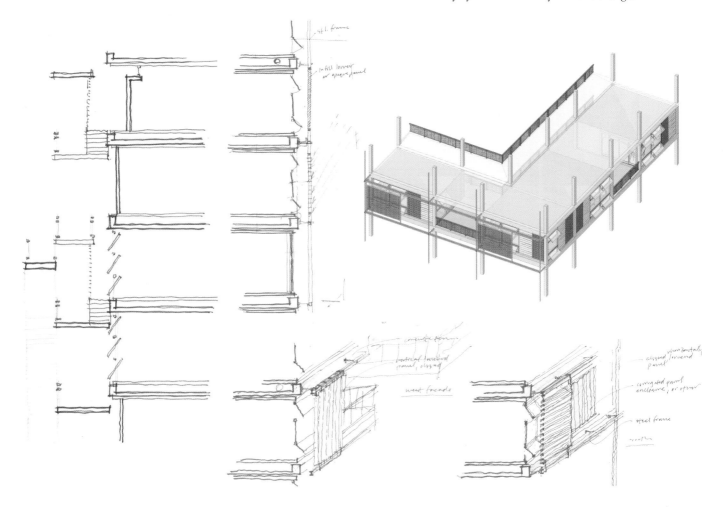

*above: transverse section through site showing re-
lationship to street and Mississippi River*

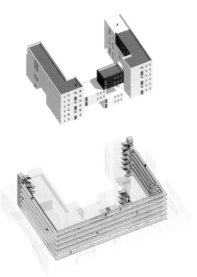

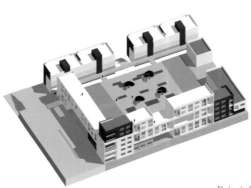

Principles:
Learning from the PAST and RE_INVENTING places for:
gathering
living
relaxing
playing

Vibrant but still peaceful spaces
Build sustainable and affordable units using: cross
ventilation, green roofs, and flexible units
Maximize open spaces
Provide private open space to each unit
Create areas for social interaction: private terraces,
shared terraces, decks, courtyards, and rooftop gardens.
Provide access from each unit to the common spaces
Provide views for all units to the court-
yard and the Mississippi River
Respond to the existing urban fabric through
the graining, size, and type of units

top above: site plan showing context of neighborhood courtyards
above: perspective view of inner courtyard

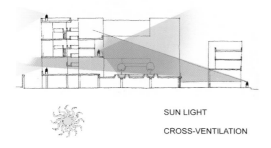

above: framed views between the two building masses

TRANSPARENCY/ VIEWS:

revealing and sharing elements

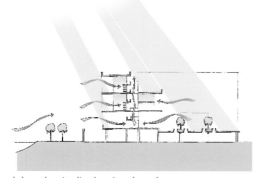

SUN LIGHT

CROSS-VENTILATION

below: longitudinal section through the buildings and courtyard

Shifting and Interlocking Pieces I Framing Views

patricia carvallo + hao xu

Hurricane Katrina is one of the several natural disasters that hit New Orleans, and created the need for rebuilding what had remained after them. Every time the city was rebuilt, much was kept as before, while new elements were mixed into the existing ones, creating a diverse mosaic, constituted of different times in the city's history. In New Orleans' constantly changing landscape, new buildings should never be static, but represent this context.

The courtyard buildings are a response to this changing environment, where units are removed, shifted, and interlocked, suggesting movement, change, and renovation. As a result, thresholds and graded terraces are created, allowing better air to flow; hiding and framing views to the internal open spaces, to the city, and to the Mississippi River.

The site is located close to the Mississippi River, on a mixed use area formed by warehouses and residential buildings. It has an uncommon size, when compared to the typical New Orleans block, which is generally smaller. The division of the wide block into two areas restores the urban fabric and creates an axis linking existing public spaces (Saint Vincent of Paul's Church and a park) to a graded plaza and a deck for observation of the Mississippi River, and the future linear park.

The program numbers proposed high density on a relatively small site. As a solution, the buildings were created around green and open spaces: the courtyards, which are also part of New Orleans' hot and humid climate, during most times of the year. They create shaded area, provide a better thermal insulation, and provide open space for ventilation.

Parking facilities and retail were located on the first floor, creating better access to the public and more privacy for housing on the upper levels. Tulane City Center and Communities spaces were located on the corner of Montegut Street, and the alley next to the floodwall, where they are visually connected to NOCCA, and the Mississippi River. The housing units were designed to be flexible, with a layout that allows the addition of one more room, making the units suitable for different needs and families.

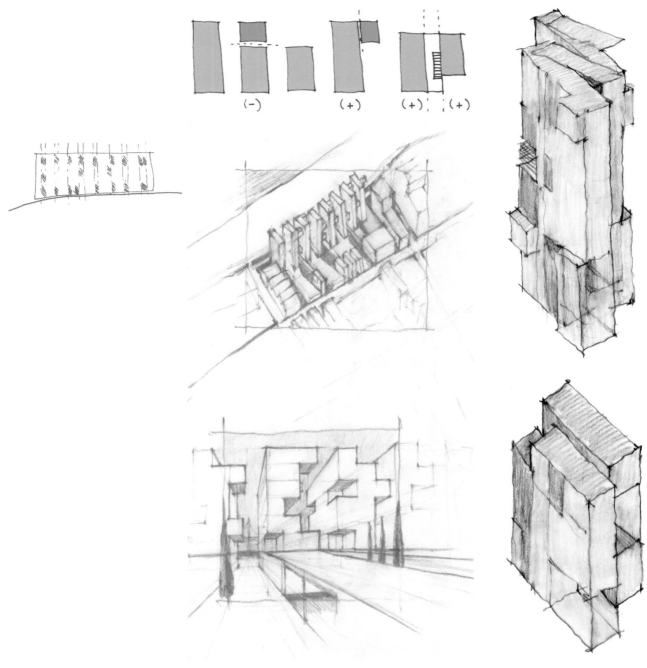

(−)   (+)   (+) | (+)

above: initial study sketches of "striated" scheme
below: site study models

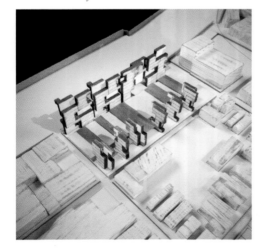

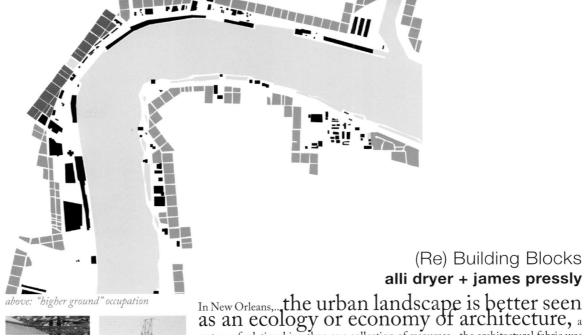

above: "higher ground" occupation

(Re) Building Blocks

alli dryer + james pressly

In New Orleans,...the urban landscape is better seen as an ecology or economy of architecture, a system of relationships, than as a collection of resources...the architectural fabric was intricately adjusted to maintain customary social separations in very densely packed neighborhoods. Invisible patterns extend beyond the individual household to the city as a whole.' - Dell Upton

This proposal for high density housing on the 'high ground' argues for the critical integration of what Upton describes as the unique 'architectural ecology' of New Orleans into the future of the reconstructed city. The built environment of New Orleans reflects the imbalanced social environment, most particularly the housing block. Analysis of these blocks reveals a carefully manipulated structure that accommodates a multiplicity of use and habitation while maintaining autonomy between structures.

Multiplicity and autonomy drive the structuring of the program along the site in separate striations, each of which incorporates elements of the program; housing, parking, address and egress, garden, commercial, and community spaces in nuanced iterations.

Site Plan:
The relationships of scale between housing units, the subsequent relationships created with the 'courtyard gardens' and the transitions to and from parking offer the possibilities for new social conditions within a New Orleans block. Analysis of existing typical blocks illuminated a unique system of residence, corridor, open, and public space.

To address both the industrial scale and the residential scale found around the site, larger residential towers are oriented along the river, staggered for views, and shorter towers are oriented toward the city, internally staggered for light and views. A boardwalk along the levee wall with ramp access to the planned riverfront park by the City Center connects the striations as a public gesture.

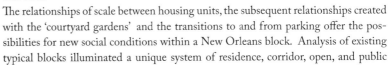

above: diagram of "striation" from Chartres Street looking north
below: section perspective towards City Center

Housing Units: I, i, L

The thin housing units are designed in response to climatic conditions. The orientation allows for abundant – but not overbearing – natural light; cross ventilation is encouraged as well. Three unit types were devised to meet square-footage requirements; "I" is the median size unit. Modular square footage additions and subtractions create "I" with a large porch, and "L" which supports a cantilevered volume. The autonomous units are paired to create a larger, systemic residential system. The varied pairing of units from one structure to the next reflects a consideration of the relationship between the buildings. Affordability is not dictated architecturally – it is a product of economics; however the affordable units are dispersed throughout the scheme to allow for a choice of each unit type.

Sustainable Strategy:

The units along the river incorporate tilted photovoltaic roof panel structures, and runoff is managed through the elevated gardens and pervious concrete parking. Reclamation of the brick currently on the site for paving and walls reduces waste of resources. Sustainable material choices, such as bamboo flooring and recycled denim insulation, underpin much of the scheme. The close proximity of the site to the Mississippi River provides ample natural ventilation due to the strong breezes; each unit accommodates cross-ventilation through the central corridor.

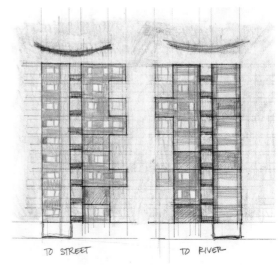

above: elevation study

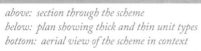

129

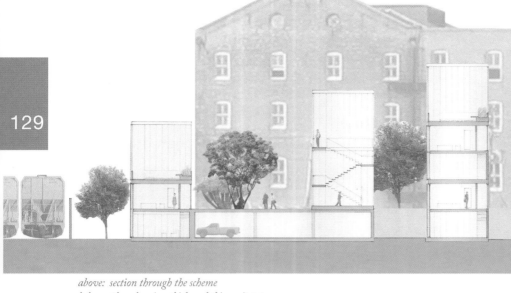

above: section through the scheme
below: plan showing thick and thin unit types
bottom: aerial view of the scheme in context

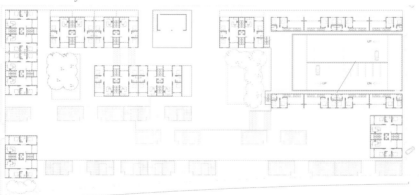

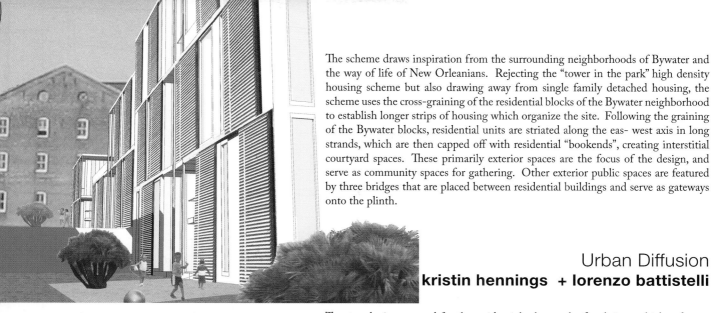

The scheme draws inspiration from the surrounding neighborhoods of Bywater and the way of life of New Orleanians. Rejecting the "tower in the park" high density housing scheme but also drawing away from single family detached housing, the scheme uses the cross-graining of the residential blocks of the Bywater neighborhood to establish longer strips of housing which organize the site. Following the graining of the Bywater blocks, residential units are striated along the eas- west axis in long strands, which are then capped off with residential "bookends", creating interstitial courtyard spaces. These primarily exterior spaces are the focus of the design, and serve as community spaces for gathering. Other exterior public spaces are featured by three bridges that are placed between residential buildings and serve as gateways onto the plinth.

Urban Diffusion   130
kristin hennings + lorenzo battistelli

9

Two typologies are used for the residential scheme, the first being a thicker, denser, and taller urban development which addresses street front conditions on Chartres, Montegut and Clouet streets. Each unit of the 1,100sf satisfies the need for private exterior space and views of the river, the street, or a courtyard space with a balcony enclosed by a shutter system. Shutters help to regulate light and air, as well as give privacy to the resident.

The second, thinner units are low-laying and address the river front condition. These longer units illustrate a typology similar to the Bywater residences in footprint and proportion. Each unit of 1,400sf has a double-height balcony space, which also frames views, and a shutter system that serves to regulate light and create privacy within the space.

The overall crenulated form of the residential units serves to maximize views of the Mississippi River and downtown New Orleans area. The basic window typology used for both residential units draws upon those typical of New Orleans which are narrow and reach from floor to ceiling. The façade of each residential unit is deconstructed but the placement of punched windows and balconies which create a cascading effect vertically down the building.

Commercial space is placed along Chartres Street and further defines the street as a main artery to the French Quarter and downtown area. The city center is placed in direct connection to the main courtyard as the defining element of Chartres Street. As a distinct element within the scheme, it serves as a gateway to the site and houses public spaces not only for the Tulane School of Architecture but for residents as well.

Parking is handled in two different ways: with a parking pad that stretches east to west and frames the main courtyard, and a 3-level garage on the east side of the site. The parking pad serves the dual function of providing 190 parking spaces as well as allowing for views of the city and the river over the fourteen-foot levee wall. The parking garage serves the remaining parking requirements. Although 50 units pf housing per acre may call for dense vertical living, this double typology scheme qualifies half the units as "non-elevator" type living; an integral part of the New Orleanian lifestyle.

"Don't spend time debating whether or not a city should have been built in a swamp. It is indeed here, and with it; communities have been formed, lives shaped, and cultures have flourished. Spend your time thinking about how to get it all back."

"How long is two centuries of history? Long enough to create the culture and eccentricity of a city such as New Orleans. Yet how long is two centuries when compared to Earth's geological clock?"

""Why are the levees being rebuilt to the same insufficient standards as before? Why do people think that the only problem with Katrina is that the levees broke? Why is NO ONE TAKING CHARGE OF THIS RIDICULOUS SITUATION?"

"2/3 of the oil of the Exxon Valdez spilled into Lake Ponchartrain. If Chavez, Castro or Bin Laden were responsible for that, do you think the Federal Government would release the funds necessary for rebuilding?"

"In part, it is because of New Orleanians stubborn desire to return to the exact living locations of pre-Katrina that this tragedy happened at all, yet it is because of this same perseverance that New Orleans is as inspiring a city as it is. Because of this persistence, this city will thrive."

below: section showing inner courtyards in the background

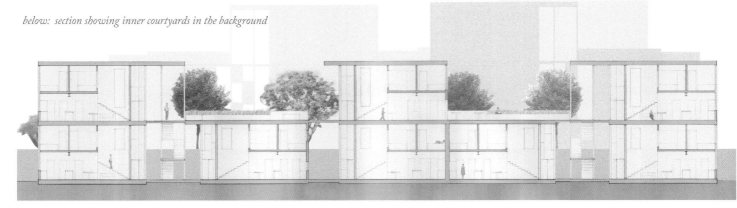

GROUND RULES

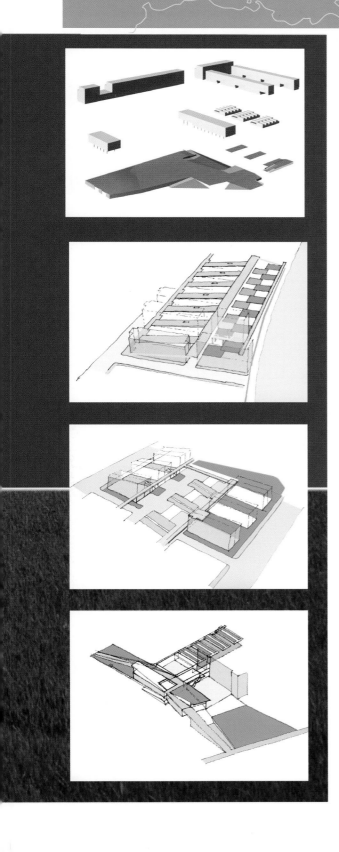

Rebuilding in the Gulf requires a fundamental rethinking of what constitutes "ground". Street level has become a troubled territory. Residents are unlikely to forget that many of the deaths in Katrina were caused by the floodwaters engulfing one-story homes. FEMA has mandated higher elevations for dwellings both in Louisiana and in Mississippi creating a difference of up to 15' between exterior and interior grades in parts of Biloxi and other coastal communities.

Street level has historically been a questionable site for healthful dwelling in the city. 19th-century images of London terraced houses show cesspools, coal bins and cisterns of domestic life creating a rather gritty base for more elegant dwelling distanced from the street and sidewalk. In most contemporary urban settings, open sewers and horses are gone, but the automobile has created new problems for life "at grade".

Two recent housing competitions provided the opportunity to explore this issue in post-Katrina New Orleans. Both projects address the challenge of linking the public realm of the city with a new raised level. Earthen ramps link to this new ground which weaves a porous landscape over and through the hard surfaces of buildings and asphalt. This new terrain has the potential to address a number of social and environmental issues. Semi-public park-like spaces can create social settings above the street. Ramping strategies can accommodate residents with disabilities. Parking and other services become sheltered within this thickened ground.

Sustainable dwelling requires us to promote porous surfaces and retain stormwater on site to limit flooding. Hot climates also suggest the need for a shaded, verdant landscape to limit the heat island effect and reduce demand for air conditioning. All of these conditions suggest that instead of a single ground, we need to acknowledge and articulate multiple ground levels in a way that encourages a socially vital and economically sustainable pattern of collective dwelling.

This proposal reintroduces connections that have
been weakened in the Bywater neighborhood. The
striated arrangement of housing allows a continuous
relationship between Chartres Street and the river's
edge. Parallel to the river, spaces connect across the
grain of the shotgun type housing forms, producing a
woven urban fabric. Passages connect and engage the
housing units with the outdoor rooms and events.

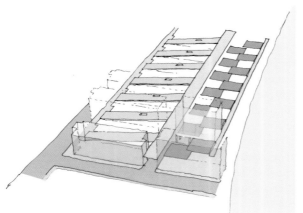

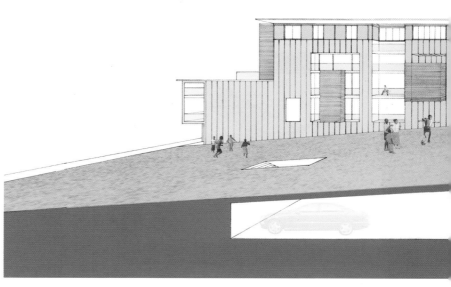

Gardens are provided on 4 levels of the scheme's
sectional development. Grade parking and the need
to elevate housing combine to allow a constructed
landscape of interwoven gardens. Interspersed within
the site are areas where trees are planted on the
firm ground, while the remainder of the landscape
strategy involves a reconstituted ground plane.

Project Team: Judith Kinnard FAIA, Kathleen Kambic, Kenneth Schwartz FAIA, Ben Blanchard

This competition entry seeks to address the severe housing crisis that faces post-Katrina New Orleans. The scheme proposes 160 units of mixed income family housing on a formerly industrial site along the Mississippi River. The scale is kept low on the city street and is higher on the riverfront. The edge is porous to promote cross ventilation and to provide a series of ramped lawns and gardens that connect with a raised pedestrian street, river view gardens and a public promenade above the flood wall.

This design strategy responds to traditional New Orleans residential typologies while providing the required density. Shotgun houses and Camelback conditions in particular have influenced the development of the linear housing units with broad exposure to light and air, mediated by open space oriented in a north-south direction. The tree filled landscape between the units provides shade and absorbs storm runoff.

The project was one of 20 selected by the jury for exhibition at the Ogden Museum of Southern Art in New Orleans.

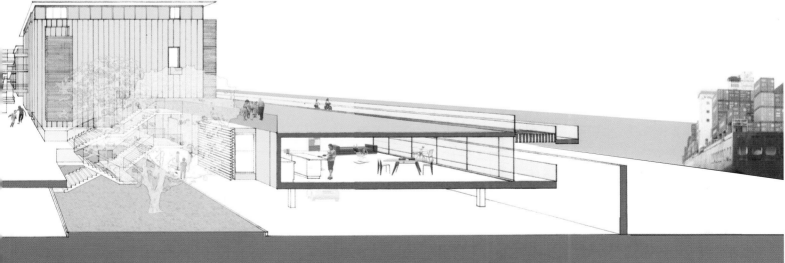

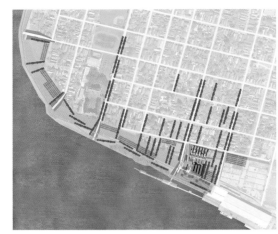

The earthen levee is developed as a public park and is connected to the city street network through a network of shade trees.

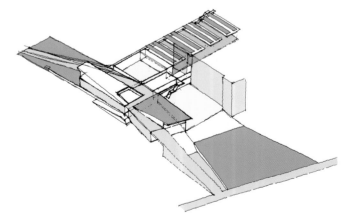

Low scale–homes with narrow street frontage are typical to the historic Holy Cross neighborhood. This pattern is continued in the siting of the 6 single-family detached homes along Douglass Street. The gaps between these homes continue throughout the site, carving passages for light, air, and side yard gardens through to the larger scale apartment building that faces the river.

local green : live work play

Project Team: Maurice Cox, Judith Kinnard FAIA, Justin Laskin,
Pete O'Shea ASLA

This project integrates new residential development into an historic New Orleans neighborhood while providing public landscape amenities and incubating innovative employment opportunities. Fully engaged in the neighborhood, LOCAL GREEN seeks independence in terms of its impact on the infrastructure of the city and the resources of the region: self-sustaining, yet fundamentally connected to its place in the city. The site is located at a strategic intersection between 3 diverse conditions:

- A nationally-recognized historic neighborhood of low-scale homes in a rural setting interspersed with larger-scale structures like the Doullut Steamboat Houses and the Holy Cross School
- A levee park promenade that links the city to the Mississippi River
- An active shipping operation located at the Alabo Wharf area just downriver from the site

This proposal integrates and affirms the compatibility of these uses - by incorporating an extension of the park onto the site and including a commercial farming component that promotes jobs and acknowledges the importance of maintaining and expanding appropriate industrial uses in the city.

The project was a semi-finalist in the competition.

All units have screened porches and access to a shared rooftop. The two and three bedroom apartments face the river, while the smaller apartments face the city. Both individual homes and apartments share a central parking area, which is covered by a hydroponics garden. The spaces between houses are imbued with both function and tactility as gardens and stormwater courses inscribe the ground plane.

137

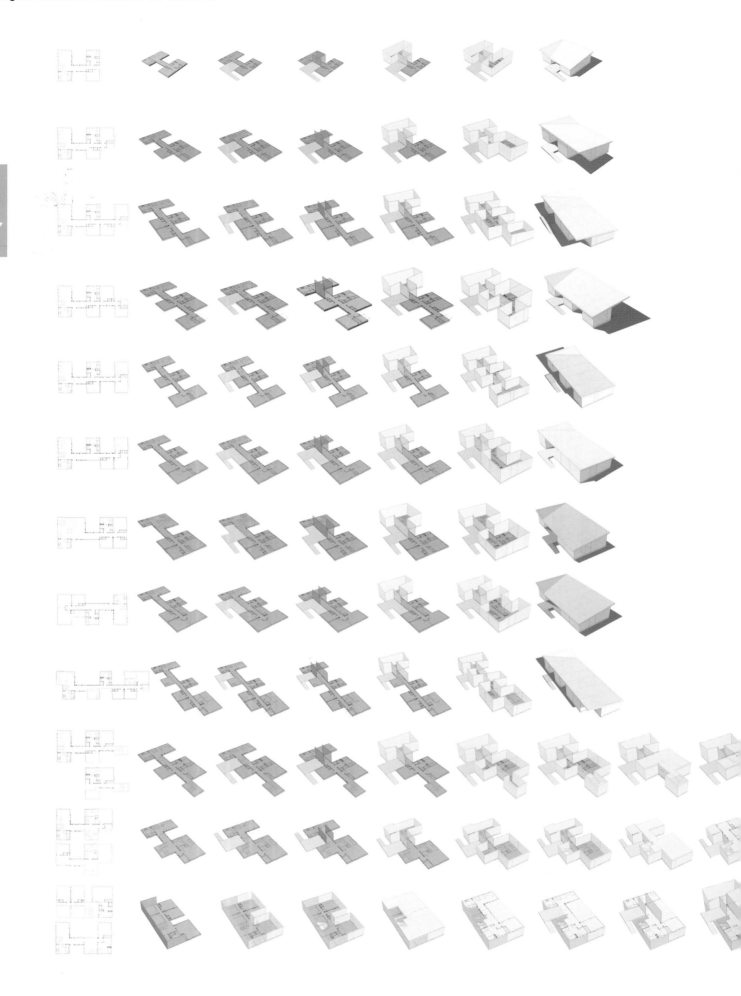

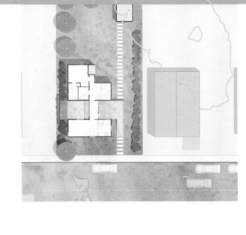

ecoMOD2: the preHAB House

The ecoMOD project at the University of Virginia School of Architecture and School of Engineering and Applied Science was established to create a series of ecological, modular, and affordable house prototypes. The goal is to demonstrate the environmental potential of prefabrication, and to challenge the modular and manufactured housing industry in the U.S. to explore this potential. In the context of this multi-year research and design / build / evaluate project, an interdisciplinary group of architecture, engineering, landscape architecture, business, environmental science, planning, and economics students are participating in the design, construction, and evaluation phases of the project. The first house was completed in Charlottesville in partnership with Piedmont Housing Alliance.

The second house - ecoMOD2 - was shipped to the Gulf Coast region of southern Mississippi to provide a new home for a family displaced by Hurricane Katrina. Working in partnership with Habitat for Humanity of Greater Charlottesville (HFHGC), and funded in part by a major donation from author John Grisham and his wife Renee, HFHGC sent seven houses to the communities of Gautier and Pass Christian, Mississippi as a part of "Operation Home Delivery." This initiative by Habitat for Humanity International, is an attempt to spread around the construction work for rebuilding the Gulf Coast area – by allowing HFH affiliates from the country to build panelized houses, and ship them to Mississippi and Louisiana affiliates. Wall panels for these houses were constructed locally at the ecoMOD fabrication facility at UVA's Milton Airport.

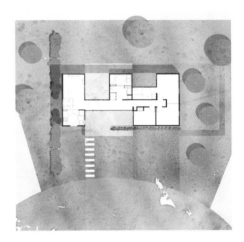

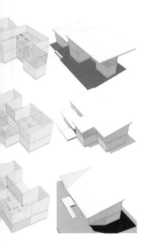

left: A panelized and modular system is optimized for flexibility, and for easy integration into the volunteer labor strategies of Habitat for Humanity International. The expondable system can be adapted to climate, family size and topography.

right: Variations of the preHAB system shown on urban, suburban and rual lots.

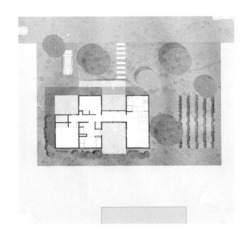

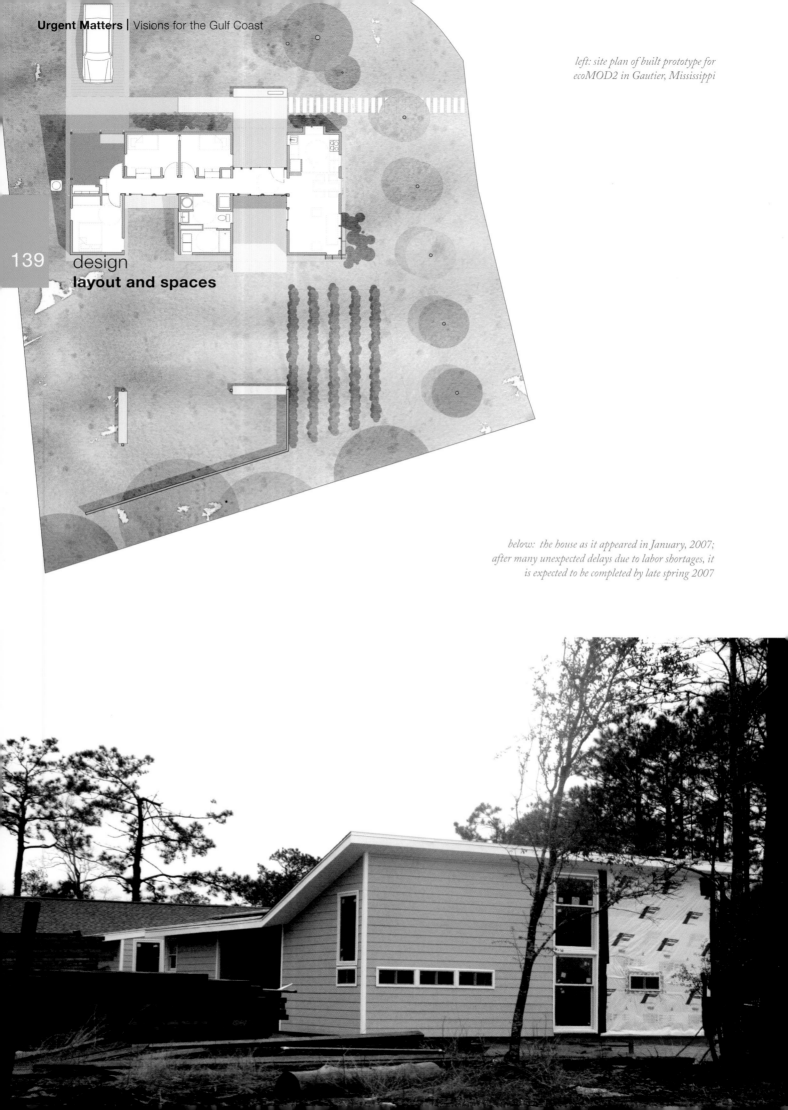

*left: site plan of built prototype for
ecoMOD2 in Gautier, Mississippi*

139 design
layout and spaces

*below: the house as it appeared in January, 2007;
after many unexpected delays due to labor shortages, it
is expected to be completed by late spring 2007*

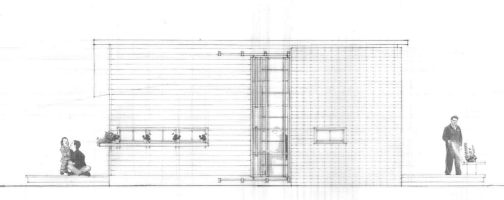

above: rendering of east elevation
left: construction photo as of January, 2007
below: rendering of southeast corner

141 porches
exterior spaces

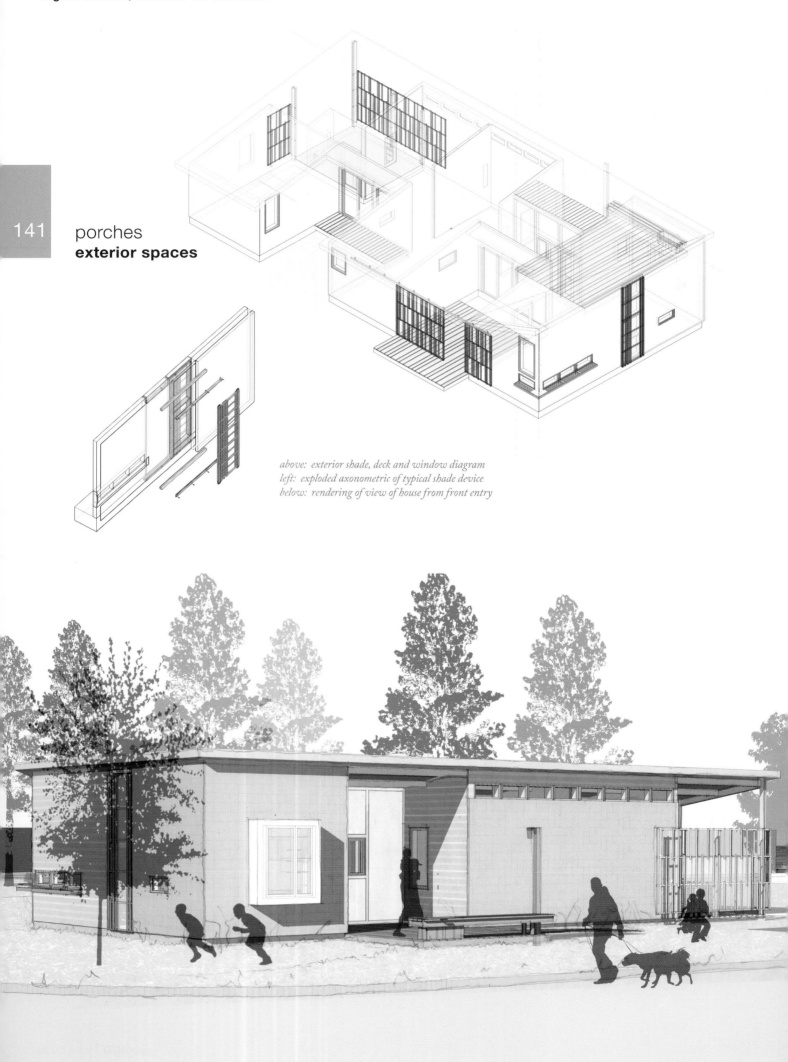

above: exterior shade, deck and window diagram
left: exploded axonometric of typical shade device
below: rendering of view of house from front entry

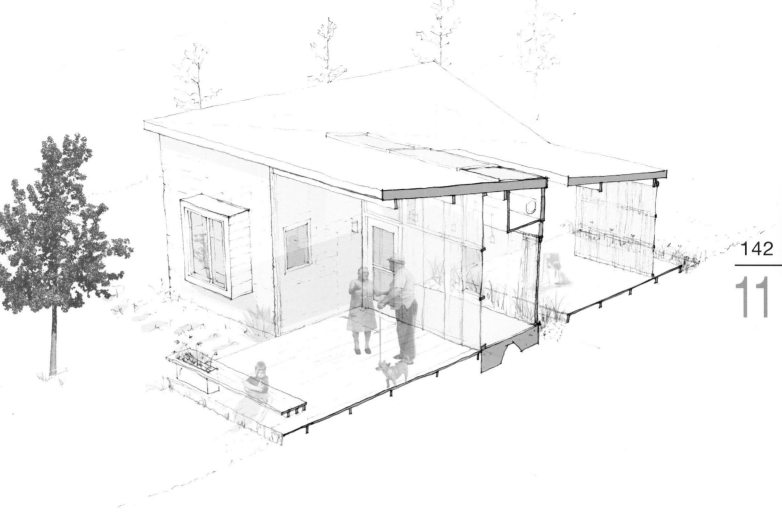

above: section diagram through entry, corridor and shaded south deck

left: preHAB house nearing the late stages of construction
below: section diagram through entry, corridor and south deck

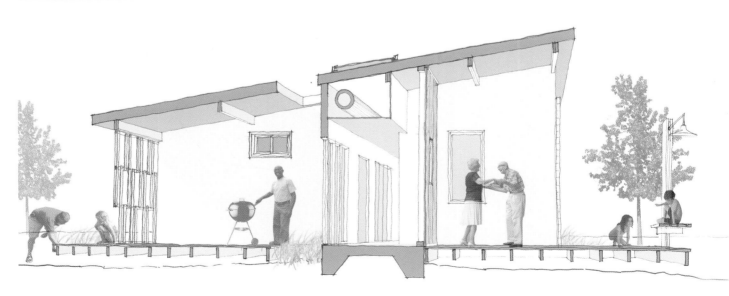

143

above left: view of living room
above right: Tommy Solomon and Jessica Soffer assembling Thermasteel wall panels
right: view of corridor
below: diagram of interior storage and screens

ecoMOD2, the preHAB house, is an opportunity to test contemporary design, environmentally responsible strategies and prefabricated construction within the constraints of the mission of Habitat for Humanity. The studio was structured like a small office, where all participants engaged in a collaborative process to design all aspects of the home's exterior, interiors and landscape. Individuals took responsibility for specific aspects of the design, logistics and construction processes. By the end of the semester, wall and ceiling panels were shipped to Mississippi, along with prefabricated components such as modular closets, cabinetry and decks. Students travelled with the house, and participated in the assembly process. The electrical, mechanical, plumbing, roofing, and much of the exterior and interior finishing were completed in Mississippi by HFH volunteers from Mississippi and Connecticut.

The house is adjustable to the climate of southern Mississippi, and includes shading devices that adapt to become hurricane protection devices. Exterior spaces are an integral part of the house, expanding the apparent size of the house, while helping to passively cool the house. A grant has been acquired to support the purchase of a photovoltaic array (solar panel), which was designed and installed by students from the School of Engineering and Applied Science (SEAS).

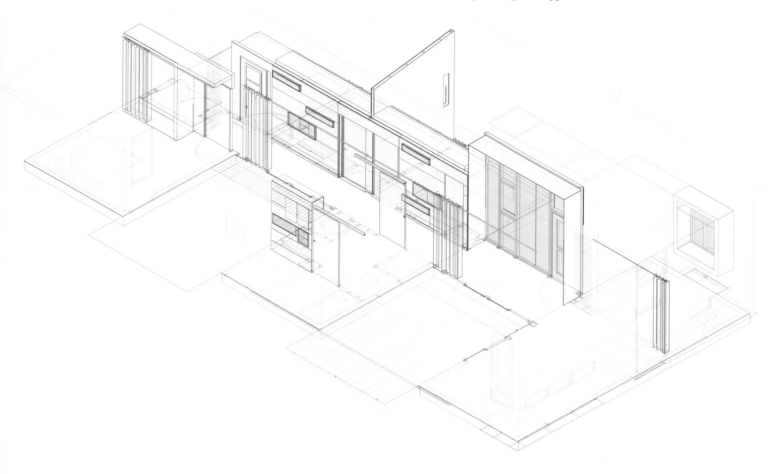

Top Left and Middle Left: architecture
students at work during design phase
Middle Right: rendering of kitchen seen from living room
Bottom: the ecoMOD fabrication facility at
the decommisioned UVA Milton Airport

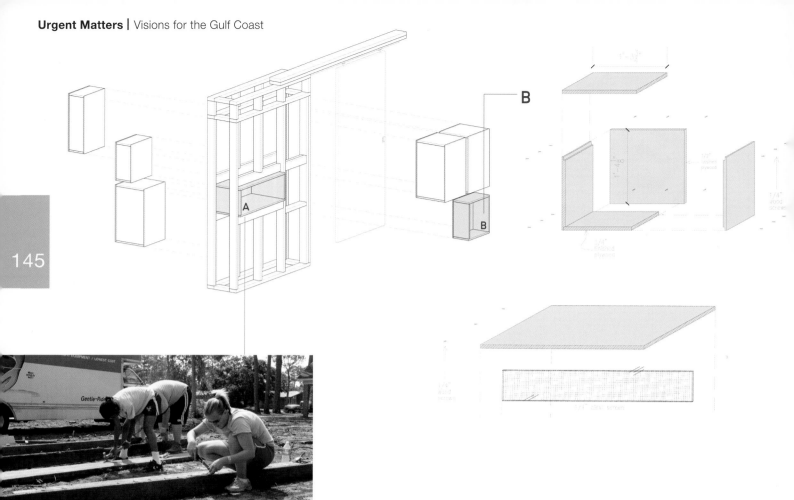

145

top: assembly diagram of storage modules in corridor
above left: ecoMOD2 team members removing nails
from reclaimed timber framing from house in Bay St.
Louis, MS destroyed by Hurricane Katrina; the wood
will become part of rear deck at ecoMOD2 house
right: engineering student Benjamin Kidd and architec-
ture student Tommy Solomon raise first panel wall
below: water break during heat wave

*left: architecture students Rasheda Bowman, Tommy Solomon
and Nakita Johnson assist with formwork for slab
below: structural diagram of house*

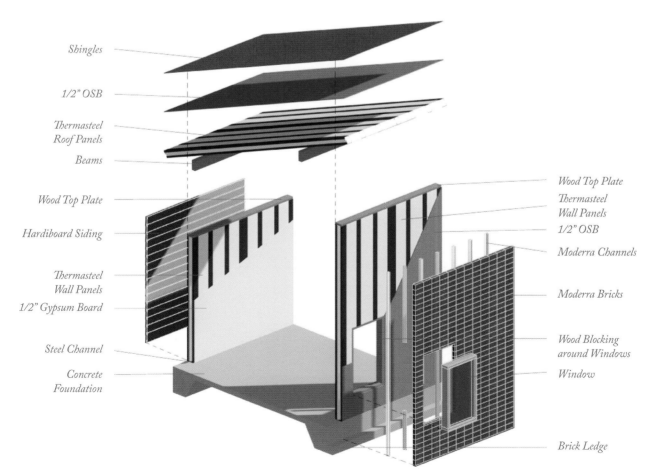

Shingles

1/2" OSB

Thermasteel
Roof Panels

Beams

Wood Top Plate

Hardiboard Siding

Thermasteel
Wall Panels

1/2" Gypsum Board

Steel Channel

Concrete
Foundation

Wood Top Plate

Thermasteel
Wall Panels

1/2" OSB

Moderra Channels

Moderra Bricks

Wood Blocking
around Windows

Window

Brick Ledge

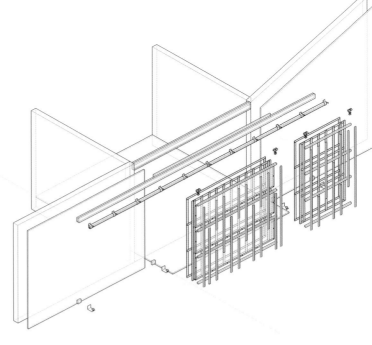

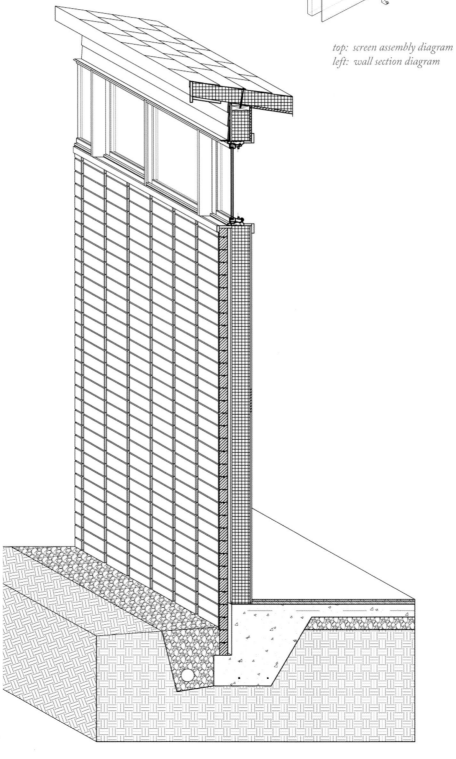

top: screen assembly diagram
left: wall section diagram

background: Kristin Hennings installing Thermasteel panel

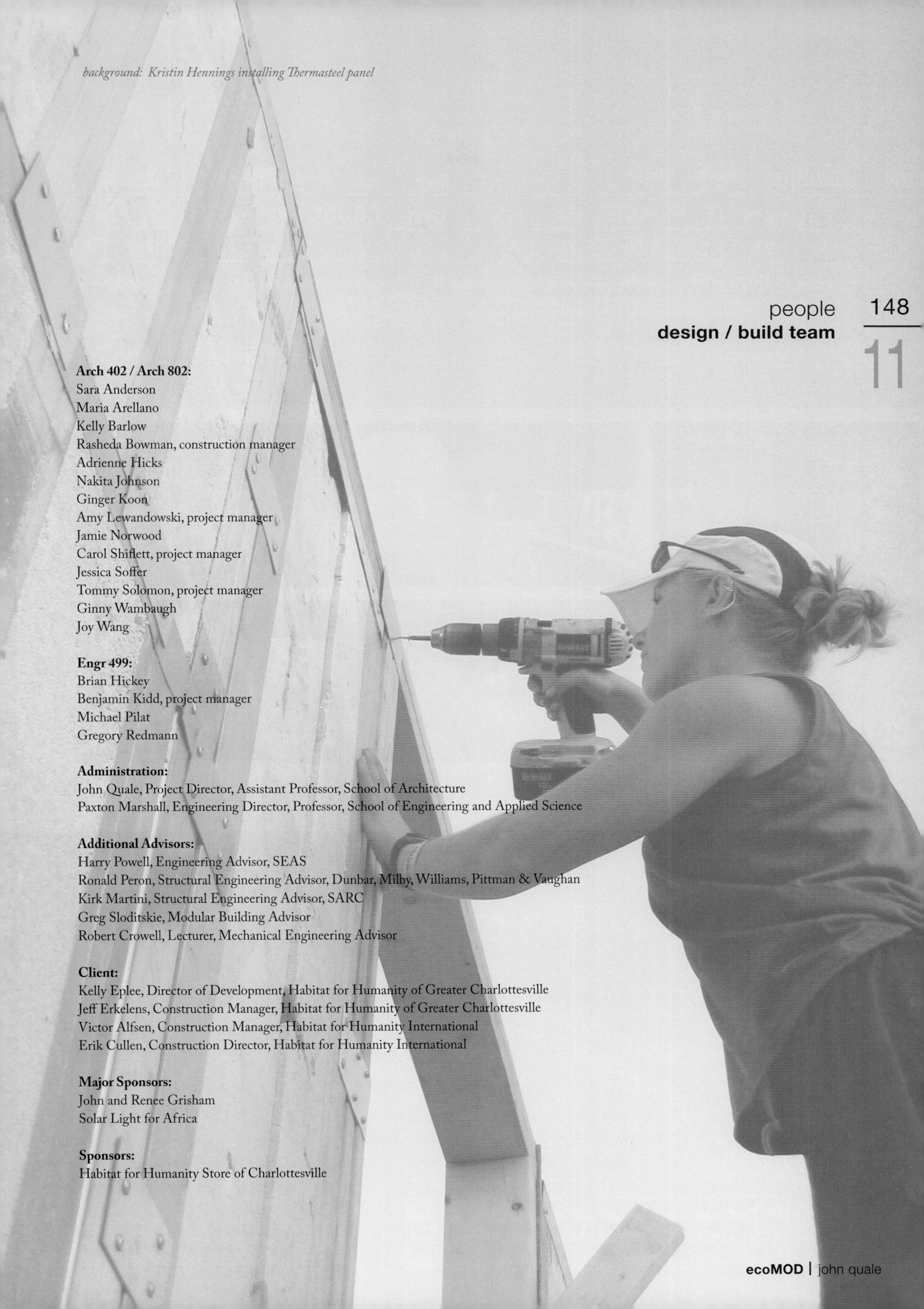

Arch 402 / Arch 802:
Sara Anderson
Maria Arellano
Kelly Barlow
Rasheda Bowman, construction manager
Adrienne Hicks
Nakita Johnson
Ginger Koon
Amy Lewandowski, project manager
Jamie Norwood
Carol Shiflett, project manager
Jessica Soffer
Tommy Solomon, project manager
Ginny Wambaugh
Joy Wang

Engr 499:
Brian Hickey
Benjamin Kidd, project manager
Michael Pilat
Gregory Redmann

Administration:
John Quale, Project Director, Assistant Professor, School of Architecture
Paxton Marshall, Engineering Director, Professor, School of Engineering and Applied Science

Additional Advisors:
Harry Powell, Engineering Advisor, SEAS
Ronald Peron, Structural Engineering Advisor, Dunbar, Milby, Williams, Pittman & Vaughan
Kirk Martini, Structural Engineering Advisor, SARC
Greg Sloditskie, Modular Building Advisor
Robert Crowell, Lecturer, Mechanical Engineering Advisor

Client:
Kelly Eplee, Director of Development, Habitat for Humanity of Greater Charlottesville
Jeff Erkelens, Construction Manager, Habitat for Humanity of Greater Charlottesville
Victor Alfsen, Construction Manager, Habitat for Humanity International
Erik Cullen, Construction Director, Habitat for Humanity International

Major Sponsors:
John and Renee Grisham
Solar Light for Africa

Sponsors:
Habitat for Humanity Store of Charlottesville

149

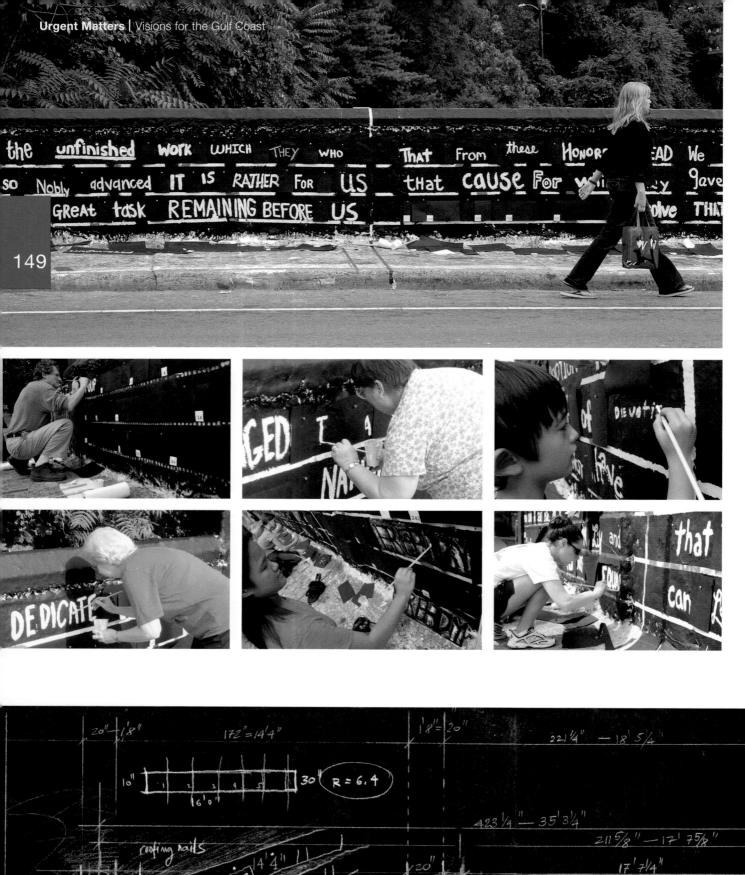

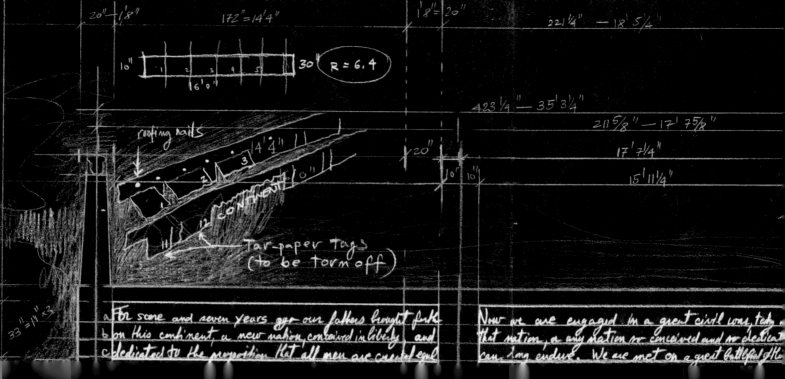

Two Public Arts Projects
The Gettysburg Address + Art in Biloxi, Mississippi

sanda iliescu | angie ferrero | henry randolph

above: Triston Plante, east side of Beta Bridge

Imagine a drawing that did not spring from the touch of a single person's hand. Or a painting made by many painters, not trained artists but ordinary people. What would such art look like? Could it move us? Could it express shared ideas?

These photographs document one such experiment. On the walls of a railroad bridge adjacent to the grounds of the University of Virginia in Charlottesville one day this fall, 271 people painted the words of Lincoln's Gettysburg Address. Contributors were drawn randomly from the crowd of passersby and invited to participate; if they agreed, they were asked to choose a numbered tag, tear it off the wall, and paint in its place the corresponding word in Lincoln's address. Small words like that, of, and so, and large ones like devotion, nation, and freedom had equal chances of being selected. The finished project reflects the spirit of equality built into its creation: Lincoln's text unfolds along uniform, extended friezes that echo the movement of passersby. Each word occupies a similar patch of blackened cement; no one word, no one painter is more important than any other. All words, as all people, are equal. Yet each word also distinguishes itself, shows its unique individual touch. A tiny, tentatively brushed devotion floats feather-light next to the thick capital letters of the measure preceding it. A stamped-on, fuzzy "our" seems bold and carefree next to the delicate overlapping brushstrokes in the word freedom. Each word becomes not only the product of its individual creator but of its relations to the other words and their creators.

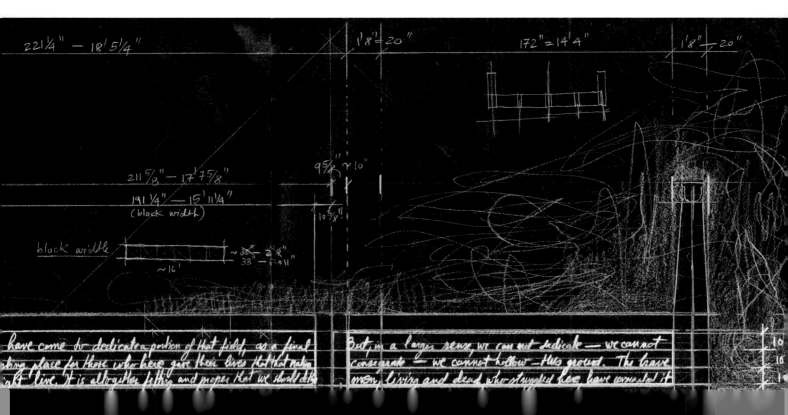

151

below: Lincoln's Gettysburg Address is painted on the parapets of Beta Bridge on Rugby Road. The bridge's west side (shown) displays the first part of the address; the second half is painted on the east parapet across the road.

Different handwriting styles: incised (top), finger-painted (above), script and all caps (opposite)

above: Chase Doctor, a first grader, paints a word in the Gettysburg Address.

This project is shaped by a concern with equality and freedom. It is also influenced by its location: a bridge along a busy pedestrian thoroughfare at a public university. A week before the Gettysburg project, anonymous vandals scrawled hateful graffiti on the bridge. Similar racially-charged messages turned up elsewhere on campus. The communal writing of Lincoln's Address was conceived as a response to these acts of intolerance.

This bridge is a popular community message board, and its messages rarely last more than a day or two. The painting of the Gettysburg Address was itself not intended to last. Its evanescence is part of its aesthetic. After all, surfaces, colors, and shapes change over time: materials degrade or dissipate; forms are lost or forgotten. And yet, ideas can survive the loss of their material representations. Ideas endure through our interactions with others: our doing and speaking, teaching and remembering. A way of acting and regarding others, a manner of extending oneself—these things can matter beyond their visible products. Similarly, ideas about art—how, where, and what we paint, draw, or design—can outlive tangible forms.

Unlike artistic objects, ways of making and appreciating art can be distributed equally, without diminishment. "Ideas," wrote artist Sol Le-Witt, "cannot be owned. They belong to all who understand them." Perhaps for this reason, in art as in life, ideas matter: they enrich even the most common everyday objects and places in our lives.

Project Assistants: Daniel Reynolds and Payam Ostovar
Photography: Jim Hall

*One of the first words painted in the
early morning of September 15*

09.08.05   *"Reject Hatred" painted by UVA students
in response to a rash of hate graffiti on campus*

09.09.05   *The next morning hate graffiti
was spray painted on Beta Bridge.*

*Reid Doctor paints **government**, one of the last words painted on the east side.*

09.15.05   Lincoln's Gettysburg Address on the parapets of Beta Bridge on Rugby Road

09.16.05   A day later, Lincoln's words remain partially visible underneath the layers of blue paint of a new message calling for volunteers to help Katrina victims.

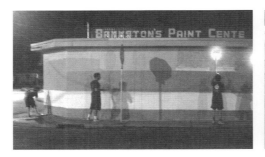

Art in Biloxi, Mississippi
Strengthening a City with Murals
angie ferrero | henry randolph

In the summer of 2006, the Boys and Girls Club of Biloxi, which had lost all of its buildings in Hurricane Katrina, enrolled hundreds of local children and teenagers in its summer camp program at two surviving elementary schools. Many lived in East Biloxi—the lowest-income district of the city—and were also among the most victimized. The Club provided much-needed support for struggling families; however, the overcrowded camps lacked adequate staffing and resources, and left many children with no outlet for their reactions to such a startling new existence.

Volunteers from the local relief organization Hands On Gulf Coast provided help at these camps throughout the summer, but also speculated about a large, public mural created by these children, that would give them a sense of ownership and agency in rebuilding their city. We combed the area for possible sites and were offered the 60-foot wall of a local paint store, on the corner of two main thoroughfares. The enthusiastic owner donated the paint and supplies that we would be using.

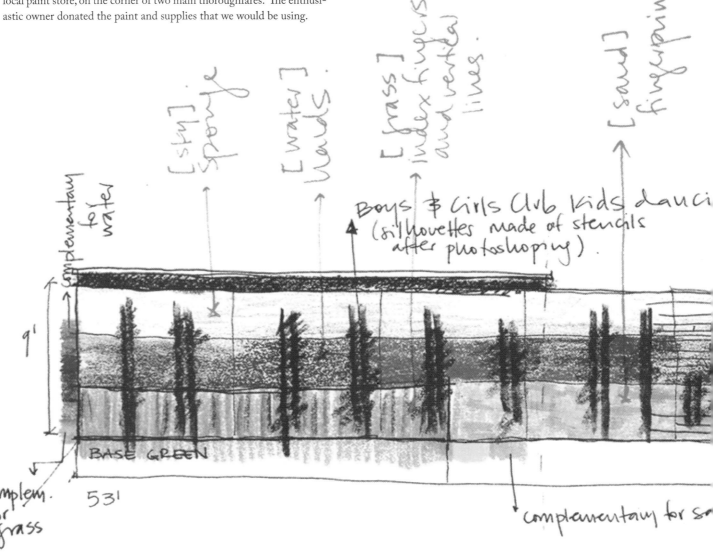

Day 1: Kids from the Boys and Girls' Club paint water with their hands and the help of Hands On Volunteers.

The theme consisted of kids dancing on Biloxi's sea shore. The process took five days. Each morning, a different group of children were grouped according to age to work on a specific section of the mural. Their task consisted of adding texture over the basic colors by using different parts of their hands. On Monday night, Hands On volunteers painted the basic colors on the wall: yellow for the sand, blue for the water, green for the grass, and light blue for the sky. On Tuesday, 9 and 10 year-old kids used their hands to paint the water with blue, turquoise, and purple. On Wednesday, 7 and 8 year-olds painted the sand with white, yellow, and brown fingerprints. On Thursday, the younger kids (5 and 6 year olds) used their fingers and q-tips to make vertical lines as blades of grass. On Friday, the older kids (11 and over) painted their own silhouettes on the wall with black paint, sponges, and cardboard stencils.

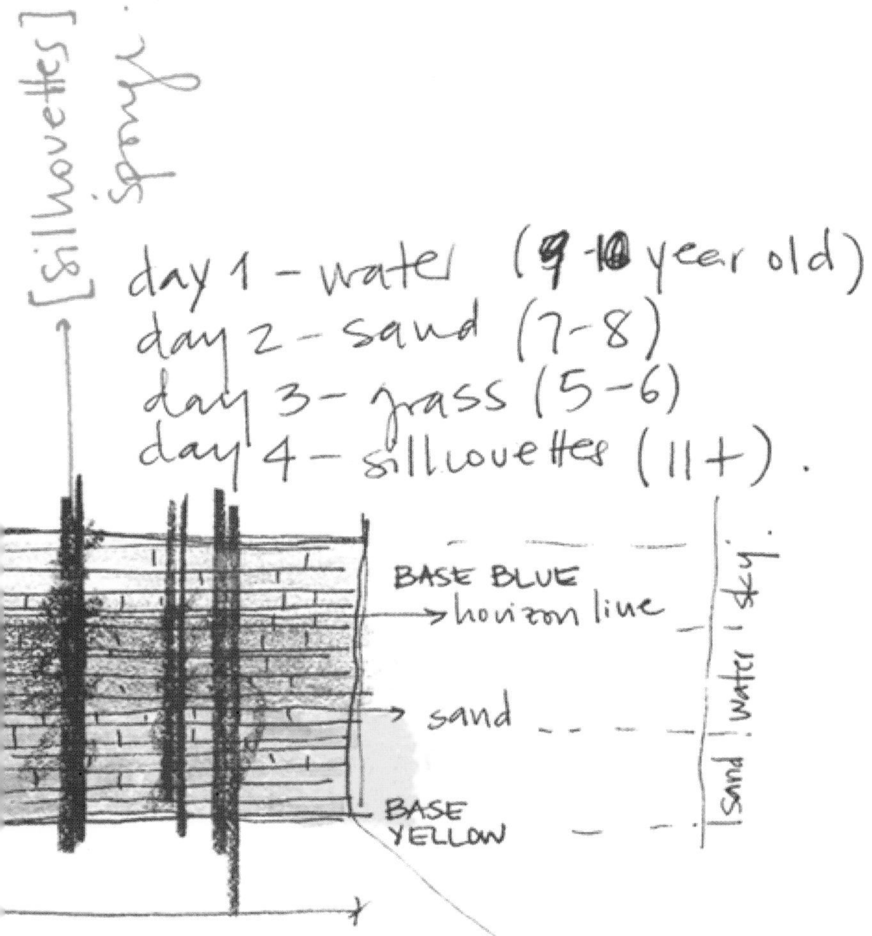

[silhouettes] spray.

day 1 – water (9-10 year old)
day 2 – sand (7-8)
day 3 – grass (5-6)
day 4 – silhouettes (11+).

BASE BLUE
→ horizon line

→ sand

BASE
YELLOW

sand : water : sky.

157

Day 1: Some kids (below) were jumping to reach the horizon line on the wall. Others enjoyed dipping their hands in the buckets of paint. Hands On provided them with t-shirts and markers to paint on each other's backs.

Above: The kids of Biloxi took the task of painting the mural very seriously. Members of the community and local press also supported the public art project throughout the week.

left: The director of the mural project, Dan Sherman, helps one of the younger kids reach higher on the wall. Below: The silhouettes of kids at the Boys and Girls' Club were traced and scaled with the use of a projector to construct stencils.

The mural design was based on art created by the children that reflected on instances of both change and constancy in their surroundings. Many of these drawings incorporated images of the Gulf as a source of local identity and recreation, but also as the deluge that had so profoundly altered the city. Thus we focused on this resonant image as the mural's foundation. In the few days before the children were to begin painting, volunteers cleaned the wall and added large blocks of solid colors as a sort of first "sketch" to help define the shore scene. Simultaneously, we began creating large stencils, using selected digital photographs of children engaged in camp activities. By projecting their enlarged silhouettes onto cardboard sheets, we cut out life-sized outlines of 13 different campers and a large logo of the Boys and Girls Club. These were to be the top layer of the mural--silhouettes of figures in motion, superimposed on the Gulf shore.

The children came to paint over the four-day process according to their age. Nine- and ten-year-olds rode a bus to the site the first day; volunteers helped them fill the ocean with hand-prints in improvised textures and shades of blue. Each day, another section of the Gulf scene was covered with more kaleidoscopic hands; on the final day, the oldest children and teens took the most delicate task, using the stencils to apply vivid black silhouettes.

UVA students Angie Ferrero and Henry Randolph participated as members of the "Mural Squad".

Throughout the week, our chaos drew compliments from pedestrians and enthusiastic shouts from passing automobiles. But the mural's completion also began to stimulate a wider public awareness of art as a vital aspect of rebuilding. Two months after this project, William Goodman IV, a prominent Jackson artist, traveled to Biloxi to design another mural on a local bakery with contributions from East Biloxi residents. A third communally-created mural is currently being planned.

Building on this momentum, a group of University of Virginia students returned to the city during their Thanksgiving Recess, interested in expanding the realm of public art. Our project took place over one week on the campus of the University of Southern Mississippi in the town of Long Beach, fifteen miles from the site of the first mural. Our focus lay in the process of human interaction with damaged earth. The "Good Earth" team first worked to remediate the hurricane-blanched earth around two famous live oak trees on the campus; we then used this same clay-rich soil to construct a temporary earthen oven. We connect the oven to the rebuilt city around it--both are newly risen from the ground, warm and productive. The very process of building becomes a site for distributing bread, wealth and art among the community. Like the growing collection of murals in Biloxi, this project above all emphasizes the process of art, and encourages future interaction with our environment as a perpetual act of regeneration and nourishment.

Two girls from the Boys and Girls Club took on the task of painting their Club logo with white paint.
below: site diagram

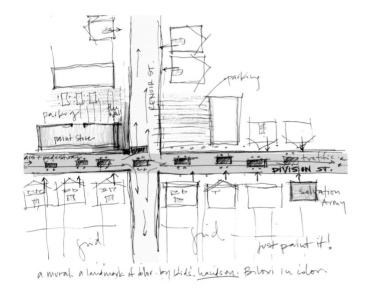

a mural, a landmark of color. by kids. hands on. Biloxi in color.

Day 4: The older kids painted their own silhou-
ettes on the wall using cardboard stencils.

two public arts projects | sanda iliescu | angie ferrero | henry randolph

postscript

Cities grow or decay by design. Each party to the process of urban development – private or corporate citizen, government or financial institution - has a specific stake in the outcome, often predicated on assumed and familiar designs. Architects and Landscape Architects who are willing to engage the processes that drive development or invite destruction have the opportunity for leadership through design, changing the rules of engagement through the synthetic imagination of new possibilities.

The design disciplines have oscillated during the past century in their sense of social responsibility from revolutionary zeal to blinkered introspection. Every war and social catastrophe renews the urgency of the demand for fresh thought. In many respects, respondents to the tragedy of New Orleans follow those who struggled with the aftermath of world wars or urban blight. But there is a difference – New Orleans is the harbinger of the protracted, slow motion catastrophe of environmental change, challenging a culture that has grown suspicious of progressive ideals that (for better or worse) once united those responsible for urban development with a sense of common purpose. We must create that common ground again, but with new knowledge about the complexity of the city, focusing more on the direction we are headed than an imaginary destination. With this deeper understanding of the reality of the city, process and design are inextricable. New Orleans demands that we get serious – neither utopian social visions nor the playground of pure formal invention will serve anymore. Instead we have a much richer opportunity for design in the productive reciprocity between the fresh imagination of urban possibilities and the community-building processes of civic engagement.

The projects presented in this book derive from an ethic shared by the students and faculty of the University of Virginia, that our skills enable us to be leaders, and leadership comes from the humility to listen. These designs grow from the project of listening: listening to the voices of history, listening to the site with its inextricably intertwined environmental and social ecology, listening to those with the resources to begin again and those who lost what little they may have had. They are both radical and conservative – suggesting that preconceptions about the future of the city be reconsidered, while holding on to the aspirations that are rooted in the craft and culture that made the city unique. The projects vary in scale and scope, but share in their optimism and precision - for a renewed vitality built out of the diversity that comes the specific rather than the universal response. While the ways of working and thinking are portable, the designs are local – the book develops a case study for how one might proceed. The work attempts to find nuggets of truth amid the noise of conflicting agendas, from which one may start again. They projects must therefore begin with the ground, the inescapable topographic truth that defines New Orleans, and imagine the possibilities for urban spaces, civic institutions and strategies for dwelling that may serve as catalysts to the incremental rebirth of the city.

William H. Sherman, Chair
Department of Architecture and Landscape Architecture

Betsy Roettger, Editor
Lecturer in Architecture and Assistant to the Chair, Department of Architecture and Landscape Architecture
Bachelor of Science in Architecture, University of Virginia; Master of Architecture, University of Virginia

Ms. Roettger took a group of 19 students to the Gulf Coast area on a service trip in January 2006 to start the school's engagement in the rebuilding effort. Roettger is especially interested in the role design professionals can play in community development and politics. Growing up in both West Virginia and Mississippi, Betsy has developed an interest in using more effective planning and building practices as a way to preserve local culture and essential ecologies in underprivileged communities. Roettger and her partner Bob Pineo, are currently working with the Common Ground Collective in New Orleans to secure funding, re-design, and rehabilitate abandoned public housing projects.

faculty contributors

Karen Van Lengen, Dean, School of Architecture, University of Virginia; Edward E. Elson Professor of Architecture
B.A., Vassar College; Master of Architecture, Columbia University

Karen Van Lengen, Dean of the School of Architecture at the University of Virginia, holds the Edward E. Elson Chair in Architecture. As Dean and former Chair of the Architecture Department at Parsons School of Design, Van Lengen founded and developed programs to support research in collaboration with the pedagogical goals of each institution. She created the new Department of Architecture and Landscape Architecture to promote a more synthetic relationship between these two disciplines and has championed the development of a fully integrated set of programs that promote "The Architecture of Democracy". This concept emphasizes a comprehensive approach to the design of the environment with special emphasis on the synthesis of aesthetics and ecology.

William R. Morrish, Elwood R. Quesada Professor of Architecture, Landscape Architecture, and Urban and Environmental Planning
Bachelor of Architecture, University of California;
Master of Architecture in Urban Design, Harvard University

William Morrish pursues community development through interdisciplinary teaching and community-based research in projects such as the revitalization of the Watts Branch watershed neighborhoods in the 7th Ward of Washington, D.C. His design and policy research focuses on the future of American's aging metropolitan first ring suburban communities and city working class aging small home neighborhoods in a current project titled "Green by Addition, Design/Build Urban Habitats", adapting design principles from green building, landscape ecology and non profit community organizational work. Prior to his arrival at UVA, William Morrish was the co-founding director of the Design Center for American Urban Landscape, a nationally recognized "think tank" for professionals, academics and civic leaders on the issue community development. In 2002-2004, Morrish was a member of the THINK group, an interdisciplinary team that placed second in the competition for the future master plan of the World Trade Center. William Morrish has been appointed a member of the Urban Land Institute's advisory panel to New Orleans Mayor Ray Nagin's "Rebuilding Committee" and remains active in many area projects.

Robin Dripps, T. David Fitz-Gibbon Professor of Architecture
B.A., Princeton University; Master of Architecture, University of Pennsylvania

Robin Dripps teaches within the studio design sequence, lectures on architectural theory, and directs a seminar on the relationship between design intent and detail manifestation. The ACSA honored her teaching with its Distinguished Professorship Award in 1992. The design work of Professor Dripps, with Lucia Phinney, deals with the unobserved edge shared between architecture and landscape architecture, or between construction and ecology. Working with large scale earth works, water works, and agriculture, as well as scaffolding systems, operable shade cloth, and other lightweight materials, they have produced a body of work revealing different ways that the interior life of architecture can engage its political and natural context. This work has been published and exhibited in America, Europe, and Asia.

Lucia Phinney, Distinguished Lecturer

B.A, New College; Master of Architecture, University of Virginia; Master of Landscape Architecture, University of Virginia

Lucia Phinney notes that while common sense reveals a vital biotic and meteorological milieu, representations of new construction nearly always portray buildings as sited in a context of blank surfaces. Seeking to remedy this lapse, her research and studio teaching are directed towards the rescue of the natural world through both representation and presentation. Her work explores the means to reveal rather than erase the incredible potential for natural systems to effectively engage and inform the places we make. Drawing on the history of painting, poetry, drama, and music, where hypotheses about the relationship between nature and the human condition are a constant thematic presence, she and her students propose interventions that change the definition of architecture to encompass natural process.

Azadeh Rashidi, Lecturer in Architecture

Bachelor of Science in Architecture, University of Virginia, Master of Architecture, University of Virginia

Azadeh Rashidi Nichols has been teaching in the third year undergraduate studio curriculum since 2000. She recently left the award winning firm, W.G. Clark and Associates, where she practiced for almost seven years, to work with Wheeler Kearns Architects in Chicago, Illinois.

Cecilia Hernadez Nichols, Lecturer in Architecture

Bachelor of Art in Design of the Environment, University of Pennsylvania, ; Master of Architecture, University of California, Berkeley

Cecilia Hernadez Nichols has been teaching in the third year undergraduate studio curriculum since 1999. Cecilia Hernandez Nichols is a founding partner of Formwork Design, a design studio dedicated to blurring the lines between design disciplines. Formwork develops a balance between the peace that comes from minimalism and a more boisterous sensuality associated with warm materials and well crafted fabrications.

Peter Waldman, William R. Kenan, Jr. Professor of Architecture

B.A. in Architecture, Princeton University; M.F.A. in Architecture, Princeton University

Peter Waldman studied architecture at Princeton University, as a Peace Corps volunteer in Arequipa, Peru and as a fellow of the American Academy in Rome. Waldman is currently working on feasibility studies in collaboration with two architecture students on a Child-Care/Geriatric Community Center in Charlottesville. In studios this research continues in collaboration with students and civic partners (Penn Praxis and the Franklin Institute) on alternative Philadelphia High Schools and Building Communities through the Concordia Group and Tulane University for resurrected elementary schools in New Orleans. His extensive residential practice has been concerned with the Climatic House, with a design sensibility that manifests his profound respect for the spirit and resources of the renewable American urban condition. Published internationally in Global Architecture, Area, Architecture and recently the Yale Perspecta, Waldman is winner of several Progressive Architecture design citations, Urban Design Competitions, and AIA Design Awards. Waldman received the ACSA Distinguished Professor Award in 1996.

Jenny Lovell, Assistant Professor of Architecture

BA University of Manchester, UK; Diploma in Architecture, University College London, UK

Jenny Lovell returned to the USA to take up a tenure track teaching position at UVA in August 2004. She is responsible for the core undergraduate construction course 'Building Matters', and teaches design studio. Her Seminar, 'Depth of Surface', explores new materials and assemblies in terms of 'pragmatic and poetic' applications. She is a member of the Royal institute of British Architects and registered with the UK Architects Registration Board. She maintains a private practice with projects in both the UK & US.

Maurice Cox, Associate Professor of Architecture

Bachelor of Architecture, Cooper Union

Maurice D. Cox recently completed eight years on the Charlottesville City Council and served as Mayor of the city of Charlottesville from 2002-2004. He was a 2004-2005 recipient of the Loeb Fellowship at Harvard University's Graduate School of Design. In 2004, he was awarded Cooper Union's highest alumni honor, the President's Citation for distinguished civic leadership to the profession of architecture. His community-based process and design work for the new village of Bayview has been featured on CBS's news magazine "60

Minutes", the New York Times, the Washington Post and Architecture Magazine. It is also the subject of the feature-length documentary film, "This Black Soil". He lectures widely on the topics of democratic design, civic engagement and the designer's role as community leader. Cox served on the resource team for the Mayors' Institute on City Design for the Gulf Cities to be held in Biloxi, MS and New Orleans and is currently working with partner, Giovanna Galfione, in Biloxi on the Model Home Program with Architecture for humanity.

Judith Kinnard, Associate Professor of Architecture
Bachelor of Architecture, Cornell University

Judith Kinnard's commitment to architectural education spans 25 years and 3 institutions. She received her B.Arch. from Cornell University in 1977 and has taught at Syracuse University, Princeton University and the University of Virginia. As Chair of the Department of Architecture from 1998-2003 she worked to strengthen its traditional emphasis on building design while engaging cross disciplinary directions essential to the expanded field of architectural practice. In her studio teaching, she focuses on institutional programs and their creative engagement of physical and cultural context. Her current research and teaching also involves the development innovative approaches to low rise/ high density housing for American cities.

John Quale, Assistant Professor of Architecture,
ecoMOD Project Director
B.A., American University, Master of Architecture, University of Virginia

John Quale is the project director for ecoMOD an interdisciplinary design / build / evaluate project to create ecologically based prefabricated housing for low income families. Over the next several years, Quale is leading teams of UVA students to provide several prefabricated housing units through partnerships with Piedmont Housing Alliance (PHA) of Charlottesville and Habitat for Humanity (HFH). One house has been completed in Charlottesville, and one panelized house has been built in partnership with Habitat for Humanity for a family in Gautier, Mississippi displaced by Hurricane Katrina. Each completed house is to be monitored and evaluated carefully, with the results guiding the designs of subsequent houses. His research interests are broadly focused on ecological and climate responsive design. Quale served as the architecture advisor / coordinator for the 2002 UVA Solar Decathlon Team, a national design/build house competition sponsored by the U.S. Department of Energy. The website for ecoMOD is www.ecomod.virginia.edu.

Sanda Iliescu, Assistant Professor of Architecture and Art
B.S.E. in Civil Engineering, Princeton University;, Master of Architecture, Princeton University

At UVA, Professor Iliescu teaches design studios as well as painting and drawing courses. Through her teaching, she seeks to deepen the dialogue between the School of Architecture and the broader university. In response to a recent rash of sexist and racial graffiti on campus, she designed the public art project, 271 Words, which entailed the painting of Lincoln's Gettysburg Address by 271 local citizens and students. Professor Iliescu's course Lessons in Making (Architecture 102) introduces many liberal arts students to aesthetic and ethical issues in art and design. Iliescu was recently awarded a Graham Foundation Grant to finish her book entitled, Ethics + Aesthetics in Architecture and Art.

William H. Sherman, Associate Professor and Chair,
Department of Architecture & Landscape Architecture;
Mario di Valmarana Associate Professor of Architecture
A.B. in Architecture and Urban Planning, Princeton University
Master of Architecture, Yale University

William Sherman's research explores two related areas: the link between ecological systems and physiological responses as a fundamental property of architecture, and the critical reconsideration of architectural and urban spaces in support of intergenerational relationships, with the University's Institute for Aging. His research and teaching have been focused for many years on the relationship between architecture and the city from the perspective of the cultural responsibilities of technology. Through the design of projects ranging in scale from an addition to the School of Architecture, a co-housing community, houses, housing and museum renovations, his practice works with modest materials to structure settings for new institutional and communal relationships. Mr. Sherman's work has received awards from the American Institute of Architects and has been published in Progressive Architecture and Architecture magazines.

As we think of building the future, we remember those who lost lives, friends, and communities in Hurricane Katrina.

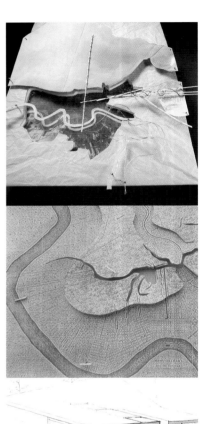

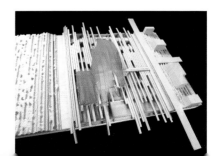